A Fierce Quality

JULIAN JAMES

A FIERCE QUALITY

A biography of
Brigadier Alastair Pearson
CB, DSO***, OBE, MC, TD, HML

Leo Cooper
London

First published 1989 by Leo Cooper

Leo Cooper is an independent imprint of the
Octopus Publishing Group PLC, Michelin House,
81 Fulham Road, London sw3 6rb

LONDON   MELBOURNE   AUCKLAND

Copyright © Julian James 1989
ISBN 0 85052 3621

Printed and bound in Great Britain by
Mackays of Chatham plc,
Chatham, Kent

Contents

Illustrations

Maps

Foreword

H.R.H The Prince of Wales
Colonel-in-Chief, The Parachute Regiment

I am delighted to write a Foreword to this book covering the deeds of one of the great leaders of the Second World War. I doubt if any soldier has made a greater contribution to The Parachute Regiment than Alastair Pearson. His exploits are legendary as must be indicated by the many decorations awarded to him in the field for outstanding leadership and conspicuous gallantry. Although the book concentrates on his wartime exploits I am glad that it also refers to the outstanding services that he has offered to the Territorial Army, the Army Cadet Force and the famous Erskine Veterans Hospital. He has rendered devoted and loyal service to Her Majesty The Queen as Lord-Lieutenant of Dumbartonshire in which capacity his work for youth has been notable. I commend this book as the life of a man who excelled at leadership in war and who has given distinguished service to his country in time of peace.

Charles

Introduction

Brigadier S. J. L. Hill, DSO, MC

This is a story that had to be told. It is written by a soldier for soldiers about a soldier and must also be of interest to a much wider field embracing historians, psychologists and the new generation who to date have been spared the misery of a world war but still wish to build up a picture of what fighting in war is all about.

It recounts some of the incidents in the life of a young and rugged Scot who, through sheer personality, became one of the great fighting commanders of the Second World War, a man who probably more than anyone else set the standards expected of a parachute soldier in battle. The Parachute Regiment, now approaching its 50th Anniversary, owes much to Alastair Pearson.

Alastair and I have been firm friends, both in war and peace, for over 45 years and it is true to say that at times, due to his Scottish brogue, I have found it difficult to understand what he says but always know exactly what he means and that is what matters.

We were brought up in an age when we were proud to wave the flag for King and country and a great Empire, and, surprisingly enough, the enormous sacrifices in both men and materiel suffered by Great Britain in the First World War had in no way dimmed the enthusiasm of the young for service if called upon to give it in the aid of their country.

When Alastair and I joined forces in the 1st Parachute Battalion in 1941, Dunkirk had been relegated in the mind as a hurtful memory. An air of great enthusiasm prevailed, interspersed with periods of considerable frustration as opportunities for potential raids came and went unanswered. Our ambition was to get to grips with the enemy and get the unenviable job over – the sooner the better! Everyone appreciated that the price would have to be paid, but war brings out a streak of nobility and optimism in all and this was accepted.

When I took over command of the Battalion in the Spring of 1942 Alastair became Second-in-Command. I was surprised and relieved how well he adapted to the administrative role and the efficient way he covered our preparations for the Dieppe raid, from which we were withdrawn by Lord Mountbatten on the second attempt, and finally our move to the Clyde to embark on the *Arundel Castle* for North Africa. All these preparations had to be shrouded in secrecy.

The accounts had to be kept, the Battalion fed, as well as wartime conditions permitted, and our quarters maintained in first-class condition. Alastair excelled – his Scottish canniness stood him and us in good stead. I was presented with no major problems and some peace of mind. Alastair realized, as well as I had done, that in wartime Second-in-Command was a very strategic position, for Commanding Officers did not seem to survive long and there was always the problem of removing the temporary incumbent, as will be seen later in the story.

Alastair's chances were soon to come. We shared a cramped cabin on the *Arundel Castle* and I well remember our frustration, when our convoy was some 12 days out, when, over the ship's radio, it was reported that some 10,000 German parachute troops had been airlanded at Bizerta and Tunis Airports. We had set up in the ship a briefing room with excellent models of the latter aerodrome on which we were proposing to make a parachute descent in battalion strength numbering 600 men. It was obvious now that all plans must be changed and our future role was uncertain. Some two weeks later, lying wounded at the foot of Gue Hill, I sent for Alastair and with great regret handed over the Battalion. I knew that it was in safe and formidable hands.

Alastair packed me and my Adjutant, who was wounded in the head and nose, in the side-car of a motor cycle captured in the battle and we made a painful and inglorious exit from the battlefield down some 6 miles of railway track – the roads at that point being non-existent. Alastair's hour had arrived. The story of his command of the 1st Battalion for the next eight months is well told in the pages that follow.

It involved much fighting over prolonged periods of the close-encounter type. It took place in hard and rocky terrain where it was difficult to dig and where the ground was dominated by a series of hill features and ridges which were important either to hold or to deny the enemy. The 1st Parachute Brigade seemed to find themselves in the areas where the going was hardest and the enemy pressure to break out the most relentless and they were heavily outnumbered.

A brigade commander in battle can consider himself fortunate when he had battalion commanders who can dominate their own battalions. However, in the case of Alastair Pearson, he not only had this capability but he dominated his enemy as well. Fear and respect for the man preceded him to Normandy as we found when taking prisoners in the battles immediately following D-Day.

There were many reasons for his remarkable success. He always made a point of seeing for himself the ground and any situation that was developing. He extended his range of vision over the enemy by relentless patrolling and the capture of prisoners and he trained himself to read the German mind and way of thinking. He literally pitted his wits against the local enemy. To dominate them he made the maximum use of his fighting patrols, especially by night, and, whenever the opportunity presented itself, by confronting them with the unexpected. He appreciated the old adage that the best means of defence is offense.

But above all when the flames of battle engulfed the scene he would mysteriously appear at the critical point to stimulate his men to give of their best, which was often in fact more than they had left. His personal courage and example made him a legend in his own time.

The North African campaign closed in a great and hard-fought victory over an enemy dominated by regiments of the German Parachute Corps. Sicily came, battles were won, and the actions involved in the capture of Primosole Bridge gained the Parachute Regiment another well-deserved battle honour.

Lessons of an unhappy kind were learned by the Airborne Command in Sicily. Great risks are run, plans jeopardized and lives lost unnecessarily, if you use green, untrained and untried pilots for both parachute and glider tug aircraft. It was only due to the bravery of those pilots who got through and the resource and dedication of the soldiers they carried that the situation was retrieved and the battle won. The Americans were quick to learn their lessons and how splendidly their airmen later delivered the goods on D-Day and the crossing of the Rhine.

Alastair was bitten to pieces by the mosquitoes in Sicily. The consequent malaria plagued him for the rest of the war and after, and this, coupled with two crooked knees, involved him in unwelcome detention in two North African hospitals until he was finally flown back to the UK.

I had a good tough Midland Counties Parachute Battalion in the 3rd Parachute Brigade which I now commanded. This Battalion had recently converted to the parachute role and urgently needed a new commanding officer who would knock it into shape. I knew that Alastair was on the way home and that he would be the ideal answer if I could get him. In addition, there would then be two of us in the brigade who had had previous battle experience. Fortunately, General Richard Gale agreed.

I found there were two distinct types of parachute battalion in the war – the first comprised primarily of soldiers of fortune who joined because they wanted to fight, and fight the enemy at the earliest possible minute – typical examples being the 1st Battalion and the 1st Canadian Parachute Battalion, which was in my brigade. The 1st Battalion had a number of men who had fought on both sides in the Spanish

Civil War and some held the Order of Lenin. These battalions required firm discipline when not on the field of battle, but could be led through anything if commanded by leaders of the calibre of Alastair Pearson and the Canadian, Fraser Eadie.

The second type of battalion were the likes of 8th and 9th Battalions, also in my brigade. They were County battalions who were asked to volunteer to convert to the parachute role. Their officers and men did so not out of lust for a fight but solely due to a sense of duty to answer the call. We would eventually get a backbone of about 150 parachute soldiers in each battalion after they had been subjected to the medical, physical and training tests required. They proved magnificent material and easy to mould when in good hands.

Events in Normandy proved that it was immaterial to Alastair Pearson what type of battalion he commanded. The results he produced in battle were the same and equally stirring. When looking at the tasks allotted to my brigade for D-Day it was obvious that one battalion had to be placed out on a limb and I realized how lucky I was to have Alastair and the 8th Battalion to fit into this role. The way that role was carried out is recounted in the following pages. However, whereas Alastair seemed impervious to all the hostility and weaponry which the enemy could throw at him, the same could not be said for the mosquitoes which swarmed over the Bois de Bavent where we were holding the line. Alastair, as was his wont, ignored them but was again bitten to pieces. This, superimposed on the malaria he contracted in Sicily, eventually forced him on our return home to surrender his beloved Battalion and marked for him the end of his fighting war.

His parting was a sad day for me. We had been comrades in arms for three years and I was now to lose a loyal and valiant friend. I realized I should miss him greatly in the battles that still lay ahead. It is unfashionable to talk of love in military circles but love is as potent a factor in war as it is in peace. Alastair was a fighting commander who loved his soldiers and in consequence they loved him. The 8th Battalion, well led by Lt-Colonel Hewitson, who was Alastair's Second-in-Command, carried on the traditions that he had set until reaching Wismar on the Baltic in May, 1945, when the Germans conceded defeat.

Like many others leaving the service after the war, Alastair returned to his business in Glasgow and settled down with Joan, his wife, to raise their family, a happy one.

Plagued by ill health, resulting primarily from malaria and chest trouble he developed in North Africa, he was advised by his doctor to quit the bakery business and, encouraged by Joan, he purchased a dairy farm at the southern end of Loch Lomond. The handling of a milking herd of some 80 head of cattle with the help of one paid hand proved an onerous task for both Alastair and Joan. This again started to have an adverse effect on Alastair's health. Therefore when the Government offered inducements to dairy farmers to convert to other things, the opportunity was taken and the farm was converted to the raising of beef cattle and sheep. This proved far less of a strain and a workable proposition.

Both Joan and Alastair, in a hard-working life, found time to do their own thing. Joan, an accomplished and noted horsewoman, trained eventers and show jumpers, and her highlight must have been the day in 1968 when her daughter Fiona was the first woman to be shortlisted for the Olympic Equestrian Team. Sadly, Fiona's horse went lame some two weeks before the team set out for Mexico. Today their farm houses several good horses and has an excellent training ring.

For Alastair, as will be seen, the Army still called and he held many notable positions in a Territorial Army capacity, willingly giving of his great experience to the new generation in the TA and the Cadet Forces in Scotland. His possession of the Territorial Decoration and the DSO, each with 3 bars, must surely be unique!

His life has continued to be one of service, with the emphasis on youth and the very old. He is a hard-working Deputy Chairman of the Erskine Veterans' Hospital in

Glasgow, the largest of its kind in the country. As Lord-Lieutenant of the County of Dunbartonshire he rarely turns down an invitation or an opportunity to serve.

Alastair has been richly endowed with those qualities which in war made him a giant among men, and in peace he has never spared himself in encouraging others and especially the youth of this country to give of their best – truly a life of service.

None of this would have been possible without the untiring and unselfish support given him by Joan in both fair weather and foul, in sickness and in health.

Preface

In 1983 I was serving as Adjutant of the 15th (Scottish Volunteer) Battalion, The Parachute Regiment in Glasgow. Brigadier Alastair Pearson had just resumed his position as Honorary Colonel, a post he had held in the sixties. In November of that year he was taken ill with a serious stomach disorder and many people thought he would not recover.

My commanding officer, Lieutenant-Colonel Edward Gardener, warned me that an obituary should be prepared. I set to this task with a will, as I had heard much of Pearson's reputation but had read little. I found many references to him but little biographical material.

After a couple of months he showed signs of recovery and he left hospital to recuperate at home. It was then that the idea of writing his biography occurred to me. Edward Gardener had tried to interest several writers in the task but no one seemed too keen as the initial financial rewards did not seem promising.

I approached Edward Gardener with the idea and he spoke to Alastair Pearson who agreed to let me cut my writing teeth on his life story. Over the next few months, I visited Alastair Pearson on a regular basis and listened for hours as he described his adventures. I let my tape recorder do the work as I was able to concentrate on the unfolding history.

Word soon spread about this book and other people's stories were offered up. I am particularly grateful to Colonel Lachie Robertson who brought me some very comprehensive notes made by Peter Cleasby-Thompson in the early sixties.

The biography concentrates upon his wartime experiences with a small introduction on his early life and a postwar epilogue. I have also included a chapter on leadership by Alastair Pearson. He gives variations of this lecture on his view of leadership to many military and non-military groups.

I

The Early Years

A young soldier lay in his shallow foxhole, the red earth of the North African desert scattered over his tense back. Around him shrapnel made short-lived geysers as the German mortar barrage pounded the old farm behind him. Occasionally above the roar and the tumult, the frightened soldier heard the brief shouts of wounded men. With each cry he clung more desperately to the hard earth.

Suddenly something hard prodded his shoulder. He winced and burrowed further into the ground. But the prodding went on. Someone seemed to be shouting at him. Cautiously the soldier turned his head. Above him stood a dirty, ragged, mud-splattered man, his uniform looking like a parcel that had not been properly tied. The man spoke.

'Have you got a fag?' he shouted, trying to make himself heard above the noise of the shells. The soldier searched clumsily in his tunic and produced a battered packet. The man took a squashed cigarette, lit it and then walked away. The soldier grinned, his morale already beginning to recover.

This book is about that untidy mud-covered man whose name was Alastair Pearson. It is the story of a born parachute soldier, for whom the war was a fulfilment. By the age of 29 he had commanded two parachute battalions and had won four DSOs and an MC in less than twenty months.

Alastair Stevenson Pearson was born on 1 June, 1915, at 71 North Bank Terrace, Wilton Street, in Glasgow. His father, Alex Pearson, was a grain merchant who worked in partnership with his brother. Pearson was brought up in a middle-class background and went to a public school, but he was to retain a great affinity with the ordinary working man. He was not the sort of person to let class differences stand in his way.

At the age of seven he went to school at the Kelvinside Academy in Glasgow and remained there until he went to Sedbergh School at the age of fourteen. His earliest recollections of school are of his first teacher and her assistant. Miss Miller was a small, dried-up spinster with cold, piercing blue eyes who would stare at the boys over her half-moon glasses in a frightening manner. By contrast, her assistant, Miss Cadell was, nearly six foot. She ruled the class with a vicious tongue and a twelve-inch ruler, which she had no hesitation in rapping across their knuckles fo the slightest misdemeanour. Pearson received his fair share of blows, but his behaviour must have been adequate for he was Miss Cadell's assistant and class monitor.

The class thrived on an orderly routine that never varied and each day began with a small ceremony. Pearson would escort Miss Cadell into the classroom and she would order all the boys to stand up. Exactly thirty seconds later, in would sweep the diminutive Miss Miller who would fix everyone with her icy stare.

'Good morning boys,' she would say.

'Good morning Miss Miller,' they would all chant back, like choristers responding in a divine service.

'You have my permission to sit,' she would then say, and quietly they would ease on to their hard wooden bench seats and begin the day's lessons.

Despite Miss Miller's strict régime, she was well respected by the boys, though few would have admitted it at the time. In later life, they acknowledged her qualities and when she retired, some twenty years after Pearson had left, she received sizeable golden handshakes from ex-pupils.

Pearson was a dayboy and used to walk to school, a thirty-minute journey each way. On his way he would meet up with friends and play kick-the-can or touch rugby. Soon his interest in sports overtook his academic interests and it became obvious that he was a natural sportsman. He had a particular talent for rugby and, in his final year at Kelvinside, he was playing the occasional match for the 1st XV, despite his young age. He remembers that 'it was neither good for the side or my head!'

Alastair entered Winder House, Sedbergh School, in January, 1930. Sedbergh was the family school and he now says, modestly, that it was not the Common Entrance that got him in, but his connections. Two cousins had preceded him and two brothers were to follow him later. The school motto – *Dura Virum Nutrix* – A Hard Nurse of Men – neatly conveys the life of the school during the inter-war years, but this hard régime was to stand Alastair in good stead in the years to come.

The boys' uniform was shorts and a rugger jersey – school prefects were allowed to carry umbrellas – and cold baths a 'natural beginning to each day'.

Private education at Sedbergh was good value for money in the inter-war years. Board and education cost £50 per term and there was normally about another £10 for extras which included travel to and from Glasgow. Pearson has fond memories of this time at school and he was very happy there.

Sedbergh takes no credit for, but nevertheless is proud of, its old boys who have distinguished themselves on the battlefields of the world and in the school today stands a memorial to its three Victoria Cross winners of the 1939–45 war: Brigadier Jock Campbell, Lieutenant Ward Gunn and Flying Officer Kenneth Campbell – the last two being contemporaries of Alastair.

When Alastair arrived at Winder House his housemaster was Neville Gorton, later to become Headmaster of Blundell's and Bishop of Coventry. 'Gorty', as he was known by all, was a loveable eccentric – nevertheless a great schoolmaster. David Donald, a contemporary of Alastair, reckons that Gorton's influence on Pearson was considerable. He helped to mould a somewhat nervous boy into 'a confident and robust young man'.

'Quite how those who taught him, and indeed the men he later commanded understood Alastair has always been a mystery.' He had great difficulty in pronouncing the letter 'L'. His favourite expletive was the word 'Blast' which always came out as 'Bwast' – a name by which he was always known.

During the Easter and Summer terms the boys did much cross-country running, their labours culminating in a race called the Wilson Run, named after a distinguished old boy. The race was over ten miles, run around a triangular course. About a hundred runners took part, and even in those days a doctor's check-up was necessary before competing. The minimum age for the competitors was sixteen and Pearson came 13th in his first year, which surprised him as he was not a natural runner.

He left school in late 1932, not having passed his matriculation exam, and went home to Glasgow to look for a job. Work was hard to find and Pearson went to see an uncle who owned a bakery to see if he could help. His uncle agreed to employ him but said that he would have to start as an apprentice.

He worked in a number of bakeries, mainly in the Cowcaddens district of Glasgow, an area of extreme poverty exacerbated by the Depression. He still remembers the appalling conditions in which people lived. At that time Cowcaddens was a very violent area, but despite this he would walk the streets after work at three o'clock on a Saturday morning with his wages in his pocket and have no fear of being attacked or robbed.

Children used to come into the bakery to ask for the white hessian sacks in which the flour came from Australia. They would take these sacks home to their mothers who would then make them into skirts or bloomers. Most of the children in that area ran around in bare feet and were dressed in rags.

Pearson and his workmates were looked after by Tommy Paterson, a former baker. Paterson was a devout Christian and did not allow his apprentices to swear or to smoke. If he caught anyone at either, the back of his hand smartly connected with the side of the apprentice's head. Such instant discipline was part and parcel of life within the bakery.

II

The Territorial Army

Alastair joined the Territorial Army as soon as he left school. At that time in Glasgow there were four fee-paying schools and each had an affiliated Territorial Battalion which was officered by ex-pupils. Officer Training Corps was compulsory at these schools and Pearson had been in the OTC whilst at Sedbergh.

At Sedbergh the Corps was run along school-house lines, each providing a platoon. The prefects ran the platoons and were responsible for most of the basic training. Attendance was compulsory from the age of fourteen, but because Pearson was big for his age he had been allowed to join at the age of twelve when he was at Kelvinside.

The aim was to leave school with the qualification of Certificate A. This comprised map reading, drill, tactics, military hygiene, and a little First Aid.

Pearson passed his Certificate A while at Sedbergh and, when he returned to Glasgow, set about looking for a Territorial Regiment to join as an officer. His old school, Kelvinside, had an affiliation with the 9th Battalion, The Highland Light Infantry, but when he applied to join he was told that they were well up to strength in their officer recruitment. Instead he was sent by his family to join his uncle's old Battalion, the 6th. His uncle had been a battalion commander in the First War with the 6th HLI and had won the Distinguished Service Order and the Military Cross in France. His father's old regiment was The Border Regiment, but it had no Territorial Battalions in Glasgow.

Work in the Battalion consisted of drill nights once a week, four training weekends a year, plus annual camp of two weeks. The Battalion, officers and men, totalled just under a thousand. The drill hall was in Yorkhill Street and most of the soldiers came from the tenement blocks which then surrounded it. The training year began in February and continued until October when annual camp was over.

Pearson's Battalion had four Regular soldiers who ran the training and administration – the Adjutant, who was normally posted in for four years to allow him to study for the Staff College examination, a Regimental Sergeant-Major and two Sergeant Permanent Staff Instructors.

The training they carried out before 1939 was adequate for their role – a fair amount of drill, some shooting and a number of route marches, though not as many as were later found to be necessary. There was a hard core of officers and Senior Non-Commissioned Officers who had served in the First War. The Commanding Officer and his Company Commanders had all served in the War.

Young officers attended a form of night school which was run by the Brigade Major. This was for all the officers below the rank of captain and counted towards their promotion examination. In addition to the more theoretical side of war, young officers also learnt to ride and shoot.

Employers were very much in favour of the Territorial Army and Pearson was allowed to be late for work on his drill night, but his uncle still expected a full eight hours' work. Many of the soldiers were unemployed when Pearson joined in 1933, but as the Thirties progressed and war with Germany seemed more and more likely, most found themselves jobs in the shipyards and associated industries.

In 1937, a War Office Directive was issued to all Territorial battalions instructing them to inform their soldiers who were employed in vital jobs that those soldiers would remain behind on mobilization. In 1939, when 6 HLI mobilized, some 200 soldiers had to remain, as they were employed in key war jobs.

During the first months of the war the role of each member of the Battalion was investigated and, if someone was performing vital war work, then he had to leave. Up to fifty percent of the Battalion remained in Glasgow; others were posted in as replacements. By now the Territorials were becoming as proficient as the regular soldiers, polishing up their basic skills and learning new ones. By Christmas, 1939, it was difficult to tell the Territorials from the Regulars.

6 HLI's initial task was the protection of Vulnerable Points, or VPs as they became known. One of these was an enormous crane in the docks, which was crucial to the ship-building industry. Another VP was a distillery which almost became a target for those involved in its protection, as the guards appeared in need of guarding! The Battalion did not remain in Glasgow all the time but moved about as plans were changed and changed again. They were part of 157 Brigade, which in turn was part of the 52nd (Lowland) Division, a Territorial division.

Pearson was to visit the continent twice in 1940, though each time the reason for the trip seemed extremely vague. The first time was in January, when the Commanding Officer of 6 HLI decided to send him on an attachment to the 1st Battalion, The South Lancashire Regiment, who were then on the Franco-Belgian border.

Why he was sent was never made clear to him and he only spent a month with the South Lancashires. During that month he helped the Regiment patrol the frontier looking for smugglers. This proved to be a thankless task as most of the smugglers appeared to be in partnership with the local gendarmes.

In early February, 1940, he returned to his Battalion and carried on training his company until May. That same month the 52nd Division moved to Dorset. By this time the battalions had received their own transport, which necessitated extensive driver-training, as few people were able to drive. In the last week in May the Battalion moved to Tidworth for a few days, and then concentrated in the Aldershot area. On 6 June, the Division was inspected by His Majesty King George VI. This made people suspicious and many realized that an overseas move was imminent. The following morning their suspicions were confirmed when the whole Division boarded trains bound for Southampton or Plymouth. From there they embarked for France.

This belated expedition seems strange, since the original British Expeditionary Force had escaped through Dunkirk only days before. This second BEF was a well-kept secret and news of it never emerged until after the war.

The 157th (HLI) Brigade disembarked at Cherbourg during the afternoon of 8 June and began to march inland almost immediately. Pearson remembers thinking that, if he ever returned safely, he would get his company much fitter. The Battalion was strung out over most of the ten miles they had marched. That night they camped at St Pierre Eglise, the base camp. The next day they moved by vehicle to a hamlet called Maresche, about forty miles from Le Mans. The information received that night told them that the Germans were in Rouen, not far away.

When they had embarked at Southampton, each company had been issued with a case of 2-inch mortars, a weapon not familiar to them. It was not until they arrived at Maresche that they were able to have a look at their new weapons. Pearson and his Company Sergeant-Major, a regular soldier by the name of Duffy, acquired one of the mortars and took it to bits to see how it worked. Suddenly CSM Duffy looked up and said,

'We can't fire this, Sir.'

'Why ever not?' asked Pearson.

"They've forgotten to include the firing pins!'

They then checked all the mortars and found that they were all the same. So, rather than carry useless weight around, they dumped them behind a hedge!

The next day the Battalion moved from Maresche to near Rouen, where Pearson and his company were given the task of defending a crossroads. The position was such that one could see at least two miles in any direction. His brief was to open fire on anything that was travelling towards him from the east as it was bound to be enemy. With such firm instructions from above. Alastair set about briefing and organizing his defences. All his soldiers were well aware of the magnitude of their task and were resolute in its execution.

At around dusk that same evening a noise was heard from

the east, and Pearson moved down to the crossroads in order to form a better assessment of the situation. The increasingly loud noise of an approaching vehicle had everyone's nerves on edge. Pearson gave the order to open fire as soon as the target came within range.

By now it was practically dark. Suddenly the roar of a Boyes anti-tank rifle shattered the air. There was a squeal of brakes and the 'enemy' vehicle came to an abrupt halt. The doors opened and out stepped two shaken, but very angry men. The two men, soon to be identified as British officers, walked up to Pearson. The senior one spoke:

'What the hell do you think you were firing at?' he asked.

'An enemy vehicle,' replied Pearson, somewhat nonplussed.

'And do I look like the enemy to you?' asked the senior one, a Lieutenant-Colonel.

'My orders were to shoot at anything approaching from the east,' answered Pearson.

'You'll hear more about this, young man,' said the Colonel and strode back to his car.

Pearson's men had shot at the Commanding Officer and the Adjutant of the 5th Battalion, The Highland Light Infantry. The anti-tank round had passed between them and out through the back window. Needless to say, Pearson's Commanding Officer took an extremely poor view of the affair, but was unable to do much as he had only been carrying out his orders. But the incident was soon forgotten and orders to move were received from Brigade later that night.

The following day, 13 June, they moved by truck to Conches, some eighty miles west of Maresche. There the Brigade established defensive positions over the whole area. Pearson and his company set about fortifying a French farmhouse, much to the chagrin of the owner, who could not understand why a perfectly good house had to be knocked about to strengthen its defences.

Meanwhile, the Germans were advancing towards the Scotsmen's new position. They put in their first attack at

1000 hours on 14 June and kept probing points along 157 Brigade's front until noon. There was then a lull in the battle and the Brigade was ordered to withdraw at around 1900 hours the same day. Early the following morning the Brigade moved from the Conches area in requisitioned French buses.

Much of the apparent confusion in deployment stemmed from the difference of opinion between Winston Churchill and General Sir Alan Brooke, who was the commander of the 2nd BEF. Brooke wanted to withdraw the 2nd BEF as soon as possible, but Churchill feared the effect of such a withdrawal on French morale. The matter was resolved when Marshal Pétain appealed for an armistice. Brooke wasted no time and ordered the immediate evacuation of the 2nd BEF through Cherbourg.

The withdrawl was the personification of chaos itself, and it says much for the initiative of the British commanders that most of the force was able to get back to Britain reasonably intact. The last people to arrive in Cherbourg were the soldiers of 157 Brigade, reaching the port by the evening of 17 June.

Pearson was ordered to immobilize all the Battalion's transport before leaving Cherbourg. So he and another officer were left behind, while the rest of 6 HLI set sail for England and safety. Having completed his task, he set about finding himself some transport home. Eventually he came across a tramp steamer from Glasgow and managed to persuade the skipper to take him and the other stragglers to Southampton. He also managed to squeeze on board a newly acquired motorbike which he thought might come in useful later on.

When they arrived in Southampton, the chaos was magnified tenfold, as all the French who had sea-going boats seemed to have converged on the port. Pearson was ordered to proceed to the Mountbatten estate of Broadlands, near Romsey in Hampshire, which was being used as an internment park to sort out the genuine refugees from potential fifth columnists who might be trying to enter the country amid the general disorganization.

Pearson decided that nothing was to be gained by sitting

around waiting to be interrogated, so the following morning
he rode up to the guard on the gate and announced that he
was going to rejoin his Battalion at Tidworth. The guard
threw up a smart salute and off he rode. He eventually caught
up with 6 HLI in the Bedford area, much to the surprise of
his Commanding Officer, who had given up all hope of ever
seeing him again.

The Battalion, along with the rest of the 52nd Division,
remained in the area for the next month. The Division was
in reserve to other divisions on the eastern and southern
coasts of England. After a month at Bedford, they moved in
early August to Suffolk. By now all the Battalion transport
had been taken from them and they relied upon five East
Kent buses, plus their drivers, to move around.

At the same time the lessons learned in France were being
absorbed and Pearson, along with the other Company Commanders, set about getting their men fit. Once a week they
went on a route march of ever-increasing length until they
could march thirty miles carrying full kit.

The Division moved again in November, this time north of
the border to Scotland. 6 HLI were based in the Crieff area.
The 52nd Division took up occupation of what was the
Scottish Command Line, defending the estuaries of the Tay
and Forth, including the important harbour of the Clyde.
This move proved to be ill-thought-out, as most of the soldiers
were now based very close to home. Absenteeism was a
continuous problem and proved difficult to stop. The whole
Division suffered, but it was the HLI battalions which
suffered the most, as most of their men came from the
Glasgow area.

Parachute Training

Pearson remained with 6 HLI until after Christmas, 1940; then, in January, 1941, his application for Special Service work was accepted. His interview with General Richard 'Windy' Gale took place at Hobart House in London. He had hoped to go to the Special Boat Service (SBS), as he had a friend who was serving with them. Gale asked the usual sort of questions and eventually told Pearson that he would accept him. As he was about to leave the room, Gale looked up from his desk and said,

'Of course you know you'll have to parachute?' Pearson looked dumbfounded.

'Parachute, Sir?' he asked.

'Yes, that's right,' replied Gale. 'Off you go now. Your orders for transfer will be sent to your Regiment. Goodbye.'

He marched out of Gale's office and went straight across the road to a hotel for a much-needed drink. That night he caught the train back to Scotland and reported to his Commanding Officer the following day. When he announced that he was going to be a parachutist, the Colonel, Lieutenant-Colonel W. C. Storrie, said,

'Be your age. What do you know about parachuting?'

'Nothing, Sir.'

'Well it serves you bloody well right,' said Storrie. 'You know you'll be back down to captain within a week?'

Pearson was posted to the 2nd Parachute Battalion, based at Hardwick Hall, as Second-in-Command. He had only been there a week when he was moved to the 1st Parachute Battalion. The Commanding Officer of the 1st Battalion, Lieutenant-Colonel Eric Down, had called in at Hardwick Hall, seen Pearson, and asked him what he was doing there.

'I was posted here, Sir.'

'You're supposed to be 21C of my Battalion.' said Down.
'How long will it take you to pack and put your kit in my
car?'

'About fifteen minutes.'

'Right. Go and pack while I sort out your posting order.'
So Pearson moved to the 1st Battalion, who were based at
Knutsford.

When they arrived at the Officers' Mess at Knutsford at
around five o'clock that evening, Eric Down spoke to the
Adminstrative Officer:

'Captain Spiller, ring up Maurice Newnham and tell him
I have an officer who needs to parachute tomorrow.'

The following morning, Pearson reported to the parachute
school, carried out a few jumps through the hole of a mock
Whitely fuselage on to some coconut matting and was then
issued with a parachute. He was helped into the harness and
waited with a group of others while they received their
briefing. The jump was to be for the benefit of the Press who
were gathered at Tatton Park. After the briefing they spent
the rest of the day waiting for the wind to drop.

At around six o'clock in the evening the 'All Clear' signal
was given and they went to the waiting Whitley. Once they
were all on board, Pearson turned to the chap on his right
and casually enquired,

'How many jumps have you done?' The officer, Major
M. R. J. Hope Thomson, replied,

'About twenty or thirty.' Swallowing uncomfortably, Pearson turned to Sergeant-Major Dawes on his left and repeated
the question.

'About fifty,' said Dawes.

Pearson then told them that this was his first. Dawes, who
helped run the parachuting at Knutsford was flabbergasted.
He told Pearson to change places with him so he could show
him what to do. The jump was 'Slow Pairs' and Dawes and
Pearson were numbered 7 and 8. Eventually their time came
and they sat with their feet dangling through the special hole
in the floor of the aircraft. Dawes tapped Pearson on the
shoulder and out he went. He floated down, landing like a

sack of potatoes, but was able to stand up. As he picked himself off the ground, there was a photographer from *Picture Post* recording the moment.

Having completed another two descents, he was awarded his 'wings' and returned to the Battalion. Their training was much more advanced than anything he had done with 6 HLI. They carried out numerous night exercises, often as 'enemy' against the Home Guard. After three months the Battalion moved to Hardwick Hall. There everyone was sent away on specialist courses and Eric Down took the officers on a number of TEWTs, (Tactical Exercises Without Troops).

In the summer of 1941, the whole Battalion moved to Bulford, where it remained until it moved to North Africa at the end of October, 1942. Pearson's tenure as Second-in-Command was short-lived due to a rather wild night in Salisbury, when he and his great chum, Peter Cleasby-Thompson, decided that the town needed livening up. The following day both he and Cleasby-Thompson were given a severe dressing-down and 28 days confined to camp by Down. But, as Pearson turned to leave the office. Down remarked,

'I wouldn't worry overmuch. You'll be commanding this Battalion one day.' Pearson looked surprised as he saluted and marched out. Major James Hill came in as Second-in-Command, but soon took over as Commanding Officer when Down went to command the newly created 2nd Parachute Brigade. Pearson, his luck still holding, took over as Second-in-Command once again.

Into Africa

In November, 1942, the Americans landed in North Africa. The intention was to stretch the German forces, commanded by General von Arnim, to the utmost, both sides realizing that whoever held Tunis held North Africa. Lieutenant-General Anderson, commanding the British 1st Army, had the 1st Parachute Brigade at his disposal. His mission was to press on as fast as possible and capture Bizerta and Tunis. The 1st Parachute Brigade's task was to drop some 400 miles forward of the Allied lines and link up with the French. The 1st Parchute Battalion, as part of the Parachute Brigade, was to move to North Africa by sea.

They left on 29 October, 1942 and after twelve hours found themselves at the King George V dock on Clydeside and were ordered to embark on a former Union-Castle liner, the *Arundel Castle*.

Embarkation was not the easy operation it appeared to be on paper. When all the men had embarked with all their kit, conditions were found to be extremely cramped, with no room to sling hammocks or move about. However, after some rapid thinking and 'a supreme effort by everyone on board, a form of shifts was devised and the ship was able to settle down to some form of routine.' Everyone had to sleep, eat and exercise in rotation.

For ten days they sailed south towards the Mediterranean. The greatest problem was keeping the men at a peak of physical fitness and ready for the landings, for they knew that they might be pitched into battle almost as soon as landed. The Commanding Officer, James Hill, organized non-stop PT and marching drill on the upper deck.

When the ship was about four days out at sea the Captain received a signal ordering him to issue a number of sealed envelopes given to him earlier. These were the orders for the forthcoming operation. The 1st Parachute Battalion was to seize El Aquina aerodrome at Tunis and make plans for the capture of Setif. On 7 November, it was announced on the wireless that the invasion of North Africa had begun, code-named Operation TORCH. James Hill recorded in his diary that 'the enthusiasm of the men who up to this time had been kept in complete ignorance as to their destination and task, knew no bounds'.

On the afternoon of 12 November they disembarked at Algiers and 'spent the night bivouacking in the local Botanical Gardens where a heavy storm soaked us all to the skin'. During the night, Hill received a message to say that the Battalion must be prepared to take off on a mission from Maison Blanche aerodrome, twelve miles from Algiers, in forty-eight hours time. Soon after, Hill was informed that the Tunis and Setif operations were off and that he should plan instead for operations in the Beja area.

Pearson, still Second-in-Command of the Battalion, was responsible for organizing the packing of parachute containers and supervising their subseqent loading on to the aircraft. He and his men worked all night. Hill had already said that he could not take the whole Battalion on the initial drop due to insufficient aircraft, so Pearson and his fifty men would have to stay behind and follow on later. The men accepted this and worked with superhuman energy to ensure that the rest of the Battalion got away. Pearson said later that, after working so hard, his men 'were fit for nothing but sleep and would have been no use on the drop'.

Hill was sent for by General Anderson and given his orders, which would have delighted the heart of any young commanding officer:
1. Hold the road junction in Beja covering the routes from Bizerta and Tunis.
2. Bring the French Army in on our side.
3. Harry the enemy wherever you may find him.

The Battalion took off in twenty-eight Dakota aircraft on the morning of 15 November, escorted by four American

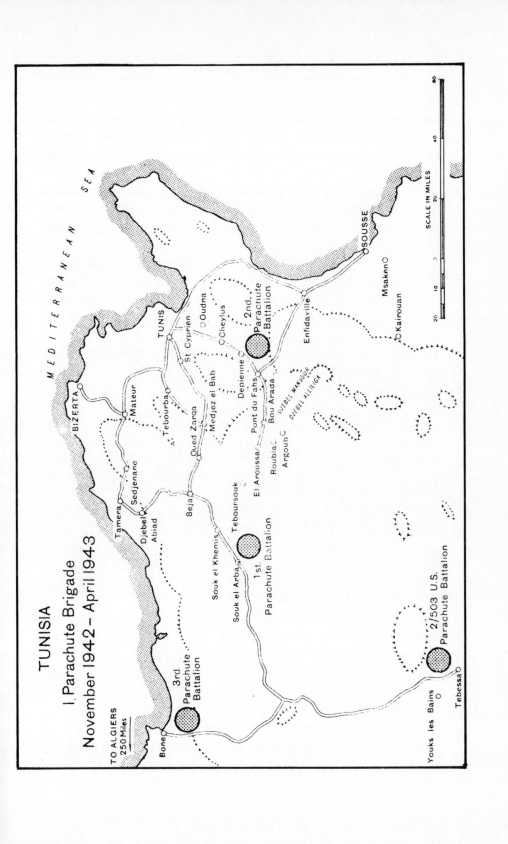

TUNISIA
I. Parachute Brigade
November 1942 – April 1943

MEDITERRANEAN SEA

SCALE IN MILES

TO ALGIERS
250 Miles

SOUSSE

Msaken○

Kairouan○

Enfidaville

Oudna○
○Cheylus
2nd.
Parachute
Battalion

St Cyprien
○Depienne
Medjez el Bab
Pont du Fahs
Bou Arada
DJEBEL MANSOUR
DJEBEL ALLILIGA
Roubia○
Argoub○
El Aroussa

TUNIS

Tebourba
Oued Zarqa
Mateur

BIZERTA

Tamera
Sedjenane
Djebel
Abiad
Beja

Souk el Khemis
Souk el Arba
Teboursouk
1st.
Parachute Battalion

3rd
Parachute
Battalion

Bone○

2/503 U.S.
Parachute Battalion

Youks les Bains
○
Tebessa○

Lightning fighters, which was fortunate as they were able to drive off German Messerschmitts who tried to attack the convoy. However, the aircraft were forced to return to base owing to low cloud on the mountains as they approached Tunisia.

General Anderson, who knew little about the use of airborne forces and wished to be rid of them, came to see Hill on the aerodrome and said that they must try again tomorrow and that, if confronted by clouds, they were to land as near to the enemy as they could get. If cloudy conditions persisted, Hill decided to land on the beach.

The following morning they tried again. Some men still had to stay behind, but this time Pearson was able to go. Even so, as the aircraft were taxiing for take-off, about two dozen men who had been ordered to stay behind, suddenly ran after the aircraft. Clutching a weapon in one hand and a parachute in the other, they made for the open doors of the aircraft and willing hands dragged them on board.

Maps were almost non-existent; Hill and Pearson had the only two, but these were no good for planning purposes as they were quarter-inch-to-the-mile French motoring maps! The drop zone was to be decided by Hill from the air. The remaining aircraft, with no intercom, were to fly in line astern and, immediately they saw parachutists drop from the leading aircraft, they were to follow on arrival over the same spot. This was a most unorthodox method of arriving on a drop zone, but the Battalion successfully floated down to earth on the outskirts of the small town of Souk el Arba.

The paratroopers were prepared for immediate action. For, although they were dropping on to French colonial territory, they were not at all certain of their welcome. The Vichy-French authorities were not enthusiastic about finding the war on their doorstep, and still had to make up their minds on whose side they would fight.

The Battalion's only fatality was Private Webster, whose rigging lines throttled him in midair. Major Sir Richard des Voeux, the Liaison Officer, broke his leg on landing and four men were slightly injured by the accidental discharge of a Sten gun.

Pearson was responsible for ensuring that Private Webster received a proper burial. Some three thousand people turned up to attend the funeral and, as was the custom in North Africa, Pearson had to shake the hand of each one at the end of the service.

The Battalion moved immediately from Souk el Arba to Beja, about thirty miles to the north-east, using requisitioned trucks and steam wagons for the heavy equipment. At Beja the French were very nervous. They had a German Army delegation at their Headquarters and had received orders from the French Government in Algiers to keep both the British and the Germans out. This picturesque town, backed by a high cliff with storks resting in the rooftops of the white houses, was a vital road and rail junction on the route to both Tunis and Bizerta. The Germans were anxious to move in.

It was essential to keep the French in darkness as to the limited size of the British force and the Battalion were therefore confined to the hill at the back of the town. Unprepared for the bitter cold of the desert night, the paratroopers spent the first night up on the hill outside the town trying to keep warm. The next day four of them developed pneumonia.

Hill had to use bluff, both as to the size of his force, their anti-tank capability and the early arrival of 'La Grande Armée Britannique avec les chars'. He finally persuaded the French commander, who was sympathetic, to let his force take over the key road area at the entrance to the town, occupied by a French Regiment of some 1,800 men. The Germans made it clear that if the British did so they would immediately bomb the town. In order that the French would not realize that the Regiment was being relieved by so small a number, Hill said that they were trained to take over in darkness and it was agreed that they should do so the following night.

In order to further mislead all concerned when taking over the French positions, Hill marched his Battalion twice through the town – once in steel helmets and once in red berets.

They also built a secret-looking anti-tank weapon which was, in fact, airborne trolleys with medical supplies covered in ground sheets. As a result both the French and German commanders were effectively misled as to the size of the British forces. Hill's Battalion numbered only 525 men.

After taking over the French positions, Hill was informed that a column consisting of four scout cars and four 8-wheel German armoured cars regularly visited the French lines at 1100 hours in the morning near Sidi N'Sir and exchanged cigarettes with their opposite numbers. After some difficulty the French were persuaded to allow Major Peter Cleasby-Thompson to take his company through their mine fields and lay up in a farm to ambush the German column.

The Germans passed the ambushers who crept from their hiding place, laid mines on the road and then went back to their positions to await the return of the patrol. After several hours a steady rumble of approaching vehicles told Peter Cleasby-Thompson that the enemy were on their way home. The first car crossed the mines and nothing happened. Suddenly there was the sound of an explosion. The second vehicle in the convoy had triggered off a mine and been blown up. The lead car braked to a halt and began to reverse to the second vehicle, thinking that the noise was that of a tyre bursting. It too hit a mine and the ambush was soon over. This action was entirely successful and Cleasby-Thompson returned with two scout cars and eight German soldiers who, contrary to the Geneva Convention, Hill paraded through the town. This was immediately followed by a severe bombing of the town by Stukas.

For this effective ambush, Major Cleasby-Thompson and Lieutenant Phillip Mellor were awarded the Military Cross and Company Sergeant-Major Steadman and Sergeant Ryan the Military Medal.

From all information received it was obvious that the Germans wished to cross over the river and through the French lines at Medjez el Bab. In order to put up a show of strength Hill moved the Battalion, less one company left at the crossroads at Beja, to Medjez el Bab.

One morning Pearson stood by the river facing the German positions in conference with the French commander. Suddenly there was the sound of boots on the bridge and Pearson swung round to see a German officer striding towards him. He reached for his revolver, but the Frenchman restrained him.

'You must not hurt him,' he said. 'We have an agreement. If we don't shoot at them, they won't shoot at us.'

'That's a hell of a way to run a war,' exclaimed Pearson.

'Please,' said the Frenchman. 'Will you excuse me?' He turned to greet the German and Pearson reluctantly withdrew round a corner.

'I should have slugged him when I had a chance. That would have started the war all right!' Pearson said later.

However, pressure now appeared to be building up on the Bizerta road to the north-east, so Hill left one platoon, commanded by Lieutenant Stan Wandless, sharing the French positions at the western end of the bridge, and took the Battalion to Beja. He also left a gunner liaison officer, who spoke excellent French, with the French Divisional Commander at Medjez el Bab.

The German Minister to the Bey of Tunis then visited the French Divisional Commander and demanded permission to cross the bridge. The fat German sweated profusely as negotiations reached stalemate. Every few minutes he would take his handkerchief and wipe his red brow as the talks seemed to regress even further.

After two hours of argument the French general became offended and told the German Minister to leave. The latter indignantly said that his troops would cross the bridge at 1100 hours the next morning. As instructed, the parachute platoon started firing at the Germans and the French then joined in. Three members of Wandless's platoon were wounded as well as seventy French soldiers. The French Army was now committed to the Allies' side and the platoon was brought back to join the rest of the Battalion.

Then disaster struck. On 20 November, a patrol, commanded by Captain Mick Stewart, was ambushed by German *Fallschirmjäger* at Oued Zarqa. Trapped in the open. Stewart's patrol fought fiercely against overwhelming odds. His last command was: 'Fight to the last round.'

The German paratroopers came in with the bayonet. Three times they charged Stewart's patrol and each time there were fewer paratroopers and fewer Germans.

The paratroopers were finally reduced to Colour Sergeant Bill Cooke, a veteran ex-Foreign Legionnaire, and four men. Cooke was wounded several times before being over-run and captured. All the men thought that the Germans would shoot them on the spot and Cooke told the officer in charge:

'If you're going to shoot us, let's get it over with.' The Germans were visibly shocked at such a remark and the officer said:

'How could you think we would do a dirty thing like that after you have fought so bravely?'

Their wounds were treated and they were taken to Italy as prisoners of war. Cooke, who later won the Distinguished Conduct Medal, escaped to the Vatican disguised as an electrician. He arrived in Rome and announced he was a Roman Catholic and an escaped prisoner of war. He was later exchanged for an Italian prisoner by the Vatican and brought back the story of the ambush. According to Helmut Wilhelmsmeyer, this is probably the first time that British and German paratroopers fought each other in the war.

But to the rest of the Battalion, waiting in the outskirts of Beja, the loss of the patrol added an ugly dimension to the bravado with which they had fought. It taught them the sombre truth that out there in the wilderness was an enormous and ruthless war machine waiting to kill them. It was the lesson that turned the paratroopers from well-trained amateurs into hardened professionals. In future, each bullet was made to count each grenade take its maximum toll.

The Germans then swerved away from Medjez and threatened to outflank the paratroopers' positions to the north.

Already their delaying tactics were bearing fruit. The Germans were still contained on the Tunisian plains but were building up their strength ready for a push west. At about the same time the advance elements of the Americans to the south were arriving on the battlefield.

James Hill wrote in the *Army Quarterly* magazine in 1946 that at this juncture, a mixed American gunner battery comprising twelve 25-pounders, eight anti-tank guns and eight light anti-aircraft guns arrived in a quite extraordinary fashion. They came charging out of the mountains in a cloud of dust and crashed down the hill towards Medjez in full view of the Germans. This was viewed with great dismay by Hill, who immediately set off to try and extricate them. No sooner had the Americans disappeared over the hill in a cloud of dust than a furious barrage started from guns of all calibres. Hill walked up to one young American gunner subaltern and asked him what he was firing at.

'The church in Medjez el Bab,' replied the young officer.

'Why did you select the church as a target?' quizzed Hill.

'Because we can see if we hit it!' This seemed a fair enough reason.

After a while the gunners were moved to a more suitable position. Later on Hill asked their commander,

'What exactly were you playing at?'

'Well,' the American explained, 'We figured that one of us was going to be the first American to fire a shot against the Germans in this war. We had a bet about fourteen miles back as to who would win the honour and I guess it kinda developed into a race!' This spectacle, however, had terrified the Germans, who were quite unable to make it out. For many weeks the Americans fought in the campaign with the 1st Battalion, distinguishing themselves in many skirmishes.

On 23 November, Hill received information from a discharged French sailor that a mixed force of approximately three hundred Germans and Italians with twenty tanks harboured every night eight or nine miles down the railway line. Apparently they did not put out sentries or pickets. Hill, remembering his orders to harry the enemy wherever they

might be found, planned a night attack from three directions.
From a forward base at a railway station called Sidi N'Sir,
two hundred paratroopers marched forward in single file
along the railway line. The night was intensely cold, the
moonlight flooded the countryside and the only sound came
from the Arab dogs in the scattered hillside farms. They
marched for nine miles, wading through icy torrents and
scrambling across rocky gorges.

Four hours later, tired and cold, they reached their objective and prepared for an immediate attack. The Germans
were dug in on a dominating spur called Gue Hill. As the
men crept forward to their assault positions, three thudding
explosions ripped through the night air. A troop of Sappers,
commanded by Captain Geary, had gone ahead to plant
mines on a German held road and had blown themselves up.
The engineers each carried a sandbag full of Hawkins anti-
tank mines already fused. One man had slipped as he crossed
a stream and had fallen backwards. The mines exploded and
triggered off the rest by sympathetic detonation. No trace
was ever found of Captain Geary and his seventeen men.

The element of surprise had been lost and Hill despatched
his Adjutant to see what had happened. The alerted Germans
and Italians opened up with their machine guns and filled
the valley with a deadly network of tracer. Pearson, who was
in charge of the Fire Support Group, retaliated with mortars
and machine guns, giving covering fire to the advancing
paratroopers. But from one post on top of the hill came a
furious storm of enemy gunfire and grenades which could not
be silenced.

Lieutenant Stan Wandless rushed the hill with his platoon
and got within range of the offending gun. Wandless called
to a Bren gunner,

'Cover me,' and he charged forward, throwing grenades.
The German firing stopped. Wandless reappeared on the
crest of the hill to urge his men forward again.

Meanwhile Hill, from his Headquarters position, could see
where the tanks were firing from, so, taking his Signal Officer

and three other ranks, he set off to destroy them. He had, in fact, found three of them dug into the side of the hill.

Three of these tanks had observation slits in the side and if one fired a revolver through the slit, the bullet went ricochetting around the inside of the tank to the alarm of those inside; the Italian crews of the first two tanks surrendered immediately.

The third crew proved a tougher problem as it was manned by Germans and they appeared unmoved by the revolver technique. Hill beat on the turret of the tank with his thumb stick and a German Lieutenant came out with his hands up. In his right hand hand he held a revolver and, as he jumped to the ground, he fired a burst at Hill who fell to the ground. His escort shot the German immediately.

Hill had three bullets in his neck, chest and arm; he was later joined by his Adjutant, Whitelock, who had been hit in the nose and head.

Alastair Pearson placed them in the sidecar of an Italian motorcycle captured in the battle and they were driven down the railway track, over the sleepers to Sidi N'Sir. From there they were rushed to a Parachute Field Dressing station at Beja, where the surgical team who had parachuted down with them undoubtedly saved their lives.

Back at Gue Hill, dawn was breaking and Pearson and his Fire Support Group came scrambling down the hillside to rejoin the rest of the Battalion.

'Colonel Hill has been knocked down and wants to see you,' a subaltern told him. 'You're in command now.'

'The devil I am,' said Pearson without breaking his stride. 'Right, here is my first order: lets get the hell out of here.'

The withdrawal from Gue Hill was a nightmare journey. Three wounded men died from exposure, although Hill and Whitelock had earlier survived the trip. Despite Pearson's overall objections to the attack ever taking place, the Battalion had inflicted the worst defeat the Germans had yet experienced in this campaign. For this action Hill was awarded the Distinguished Service Order and Pearson the

Military Cross. The official report on the engagement reports the British casualties as:

'CO and Adjutant severely wounded. 3 Other Ranks killed and 3 Other Ranks wounded. Capt Geary RE was killed and 2 RE officers and 15 ORs, RE missing.'

The day after the battle, Alastair Pearson, at twenty-seven one of the youngest battalion commanders in the British Army, laid down the ground rules for his new command:

'Gentlemen,' he told his officers, 'do what you are told and stay alive. Remember there will be no bloody medals in this Battalion.'

In the months that followed only one of his orders would be obeyed. His men did what they were told.

V

In Command

Alastair Pearson assumed command of the 1st Battalion on 25 November, 1942, and Peter Cleasby-Thompson became Second-in-Command. The next day, the Battalion became part of Blade Force, the advance guard of the First British Army. They moved to a new position, ten miles south of Mateur. However, Pearson's command was very nearly curtailed before it had begun.

He was being driven back to Battalion Headquarters, after a conference at Brigade, in a requisitioned Citröen car driven by Private Whittingham, his driver. Coming from the direction of Tunis were five or six Stuka bombers who passed over them going towards Beja. Pearson remarked to Whittingham,

'I wonder what target they have in mind?'

Hardly had the words left his lips, when the Stukas began to circle and Pearson roared,

'Stop. It's us!'

They both leapt out of the car and ran for a nearby field. The Stukas peeled off and began their bombing run. Each aircraft screamed down and released its deadly cargo, but neither the car nor its occupants were hit. As they returned to the car, Pearson looked up at the departing aircraft and commented,

'They should be RTU'd* for missing us from such a low dive!' They then continued their journey undisturbed.

During this period the Battalion's mission was to harass the Germans, whenever and wherever they could. This was a job well-suited to the paratroopers, who thrive on this form of hit-and-run warfare. The other two parachute battalions from the brigade were in the area, but as the 1st Battalion

* Returned to Unit.

was more isolated then the others, Pearson 'was by this fact
"to all intents and purposes his own master"'. A number of
officers and men showed themselves particularly well suited
for this type of work.

The Battalion was based on a farm, known as Coxen's
Farm, named after Vic Coxen, a young officer in the Battalion
who first discovered it. Pearson had chosen the farm as an
ideal base from which to launch hit-and-run raids on the
Germans. When they moved into the farm, they found all the
farm animals drunk on wine which was spilling out of some
shell-blasted casks. A great round-up was staged, and the
soldiers sent the bellowing cattle reeling towards the German
lines, which were only six hundred yards away.

During the day, they slept when they could get some peace
from the German air attacks and mortar bombardments. At
night they raided German outposts and bases. They
ambushed convoys, blew up supply dumps and stealthily
penetrated the enemy encampments to create havoc among
the sleeping Germans. As the Germans did very little patrolling at night, this made the paratroopers' job that much
easier.

On one patrol, Lieutenant Phillip Mellor, who had won an
MC at Medjez el Bab, sent his men back to base after a
German armoured car had raised the alarm, and went on
himself into the enemy fortress at Mateur. There were five
thousand Germans in Mateur, which was twenty miles
behind enemy lines. Mellor spent the night wandering around
the streets gunning down stray Germans. He returned to
camp the next day with a bullet hole in his helmet as a
souvenir.

Another subaltern, Lieutenant Stan Wandless, who had
already distinguished himself in action, also went into Mateur
and found a house full of German officers. Wandless spoke
perfect German and had an intense hatred for them. He
knifed a sentry and, when an officer left the house, he
approached him and told him that he was a prisoner of war.
The German told him to stop joking. Wandless shot him and
then lobbed several grenades through a window of the house.

1. Officers of the 1st Parachute Battalion at Bulford, 1942.
Alastair Pearson is seated, wearing tartan trews. James Hill is on his left.

2. A patrol of the 1st Parachute Brigade near Beja, Tunisia, 26 December, 1942.

3. Brigadier James Hill with Princess Elizabeth
during an inspection of 3rd Parachute Brigade, Salisbury Plain, 1944.

4. Her Majesty the Queen, with Princess Elizabeth, talking to Pte Macdonald, son of one of the ghillies on the Glamis estate.

5. Alastair Pearson (*second from left*) with his HQ, 8th Parachute Battalion; Tilshead Camp, May, 1944.

6. General Sir Richard Gale,
Commander 6th Airborne Division.

He waited outside and killed the survivors with his hunting knife as they tried to escape through the front door.

A patrol led by Chris Perrin-Brown, the Intelligence Officer, was sent out to examine a bridge across a river. While they were there a group of Germans arrived to guard the bridge. Perrin-Brown and his men hid underneath for several hours until daylight came and they could see the strength of the Germans. But as dawn broke, they were spotted by another enemy patrol, about forty in number, coming up the road. The paratroopers opened up with their rifles and grenades. The Germans on the bridge were totally confused and turned their guns on the second patrol. Perrin-Brown and his men escaped in the chaos, leaving the Germans firing away at each other.

Back at Coxen's Farm, the Germans kept up a steady mortar barrage in a fruitless attempt to dislodge the paratroopers. Each day the attacks increased in ferocity. During such attacks Pearson was always up and about, keeping his men calm under the bombardments. He seemed to have a sixth sense about who was likely to cause problems, and had the knack of being able to calm his less experienced soldiers when the going was rough. The mortar barrages lasted for hours on end. The Germans were deadly accurate and these attacks 'were most unpleasant'.

The Germans also sent in Stuka bombers in the hope that their screaming, bombing and strafing would force the men of the 1st Battalion to withdraw. But the paratroopers stayed, ever more resolute. The Germans also cut the road through the valley, to stop supply trucks bringing food to the farm from the main Battalion supply base six miles away. Everything that moved on the farm during daylight became the target for the enemy machine gunners.

Finally, in desperation, the Germans decided that a massive effort must be made to remove the constant menace of the paratroopers' night raids. The hills around the farm began to fill with more German troops and it soon became obvious to Pearson that they were preparing for an overwhelming assault.

He called for a conference with the commander of a squadron of 17/21st Lancers, Major ffrench-Blake, and a sizeable part of the 2nd Battalion, The Lancashire Fusiliers, commanded by Major Kelly, both of whom had been sent to support the 1st Battalion.

'I think the Germans are going to give us an almighty pasting if we don't get out of here,' said Pearson. 'As far as I can see, there is only one thing to do. Attack!'

The British were outnumbered by three to one, but Pearson based his astonishing strategy on the theory that the advantage of attacking more than evened up the score!

'If we give them a bloody nose before we leave, they won't be so keen to come after us,' he reasoned.

That night Bill Clarke, his wireless operator from Yorkshire, noted in his pocket diary:

'We are going to attack a hill across nearly a mile of open ground. We'll never make it.'

It was decided to launch the attack on the afternoon of 1 December. The first phase of the attack began at 1515 hours, with an assault on a small farm to the south-east of Coxen's Farm. Three Valentine tanks, carrying one section of T Company, moved out. After preliminary machine-gunning by the tanks, the section entered the farm which was found to have been evacuated. The section returned to Coxen's Farm and the tanks rejoined their squadron.

At about the same time, Pearson led his men across the floor of the valley behind the tanks, which laid down 'an excellent smoke screen' to cover R Company. The tanks machine-gunned the main enemy positions and the paratroopers stormed up the hill. The Germans fled, but, as they withdrew, a devastating, covering crossfire belched over their heads from eight machine guns sighted in depth, and the forward rush of the paratroopers was halted.

Pearson spread his men out along the first ridge and began a two-hour duel across the slopes. The Germans brought up field guns and sent shells thudding into the farm behind the paratroopers. Light began to fail at 1730 hours, and at 1800 hours he ordered R Company to withdraw carrying their wounded. The dead, Lieutenant Foggarty and two soldiers, had to be left. Their casualties, overall, were three killed and seven wounded. German casualties were impossible to estimate.

By this time the farm was a blazing ruin. A German shell had hit a captured truck full of explosives, and the buildings were shattered by the blast. Silhouetted by flames, Pearson's men rushed around the farm, packing their equipment and loading the wounded on to Italian trucks, while a defence squad fought off the Germans around the perimeter. As the trucks rolled out of the back of the farm, Pearson lined up his men and calmly marched them out as the first German tanks came grinding over the fields. He turned back, once more, with his mortar platoon, to give the approaching enemy a final salvo and then jumped into his battered Citröen and sped after his troops.

The Germans watched the paratroopers disappearing into the safety of the darkness and wearily ended their pursuit. They had found that night-fighting with the British was like facing a firing squad blindfold, and they had already lost enough men.

In the face of what, to lesser men, might have seemed certain disaster, Alastair Pearson had delivered his bloody nose and successfully escaped the threat of massacre. But his pride was in his men.

'They're the finest soldiers in the world,' he told Cleasby-Thompson, as they drove over the desert track. 'I would go to hell and back with them.'

The men withdrew to the main Battalion base, where they stayed, keeping up their nightly patrolling activity. The next few days were spent resting and trying to fight the cold and the heavy rain which made life very miserable. The companies were under cover but 'most uncomfortable'.

After the attack at Coxen's Farm, the Battalion moved back to a rest area in Souk el Khemis. Billets were found in local farms and here they met up with their colleagues from the 2nd Battalion, commanded by Lieutenant-Colonel John

Frost. Life behind the front line became a watery misery in which the main battle was trying to mitigate the discomfort.

Major Peter Cleasby-Thompson, the Second-in-Command, had captured a German officer called Heinrich, along with his batman who had refused to leave him. Heinrich and his batman ministered to their captor's needs like well-trained servants, making tea and preparing hot water for baths. Heinrich had been a schoolmaster in Germany and spoke extremely good English. He spoke very highly of the paratroopers, especially when they had tried to take his watch. He told them that it was his own and not an army issue one, so the troops allowed him to keep it. The Battalion diary records Heinrich making the following profound remark: 'We Germans have the Italians and you English have the Americans'!

During the days before Christmas, 1942, the Battalion was sorting itself out, re-equipping, cleaning and generally preparing for the next battle, which they knew would be inevitable. A telegram system was set up for Christmas and greetings were laid on at a price of 40 Francs per telegram. On 23 December, Major-General F. A. M. 'Boy' Browning visited the Battalion and 'appeared pleased with our performance up to date'.

Because the weather was so miserable, the men stayed in their tents, playing cards or sleeping. The medical officer, Dr Michael Heggie, rode about the camp on a captured tricycle and made many successful visits to a monastery, where the local monks made a most efficacious 'pain-killing' wine. The Padre also travelled about and visited Beja on Christmas Eve. He had heard that a shop was open and had gone to see if there was anything worth buying. He joined a queue of soldiers, believing it to be for the shop. But when he got to the front he found he was next in line for a house of ill-fame!

That evening Alastair Pearson caught fire. He had seen some soldiers making a fire in a mess tin with sand and petrol, and one such contraption was installed in the Officers' Mess. Later that evening the fire was burning low and Pearson emptied a jar of petrol on to it. He went up in smoke and was only saved by his fellow officers who rolled him in blankets. But he was angered by the mysterious way in which his watch disappeared whilst his burns were being treated.

'You should really be in hospital,' Doctor Heggie told him. 'These burns are serious.'

'I'm not leaving the Battalion while my watch is missing,' replied Pearson. 'When I find the man who did it, his feet won't touch the ground!'

So Pearson enjoyed only the hard canvas of a stretcher, rather than a comfortable hospital bed. He lay there like a stranded walrus, his great white-bandaged arms supporting a tiny tartan-covered pocket edtion of the works of Robert Burns. Occasionally his large jowls creased in a grin and he grunted with approval as his favourite poet hit a responsive chord in his rebellious Scottish soul. He soothed his burns with Burns. No matter how critical the battle, Pearson always found time for a minute or two with Burns each day.

Christmas Day came and went— 'Very wet and with no presents'. Good wishes poured in from all units. Personal good wishes were brought by Johnny Frost from the 2nd Battalion. It was noted by the Adjutant that the visit 'cost him 1000 Francs owing to his inability to ride his motorcycle in the upright position after lunch!'

The same day the Battalion received orders to take over from the 3rd Parachute Battalion in the Beja Gap and hold it. They dug themselves into the mountain side for warmth as well as protection from attack. Their patrolling area was well forward in the north-east of the Sidi N'Sir station— 'ground well known to us.' On 28 December they located the enemy and were in contact once again. The New Year of 1943 saw little change in the cold wet weather and the ground was still mostly impassable to wheeled vehicles.

On 5 January the Battalion moved by train from Souk el Khemis, travelling in cattle trucks. There were no facilities on board, so every stop saw men hopping off to answer the call of nature. The train looked a glorious sight, having cooking tins and pots suspended all over the outside. Cooking was done in fits and starts. When the train stopped, men were out like a flash and fires were lit.

At a siding somewhere en route the train stopped for twenty minutes, but before they moved off they were accused of stealing seventy-five sacks of grain. Captain O'Brien, the Adjutant, notes: 'This we denied as being impossible . . . even for us!'

They eventually arrived at Boufarik on 11 January, and marched to a large farm at St Marguerite on the outskirts of the town, where they moved into excellent billets. Several hospital cases had returned and were welcomed back with enthusiasm. The Battalion returned to training, programmes were produced and a mortar cadre put into operation.

The next day, 12 January, Pearson was lighting his blackened pipe, and, as he disappeared in a cloud of smoke, the door of his room opened. Through the smoke he could see a smartly dressed, distinguished-looking officer called Lieutenant-Colonel Gofton-Salmond, who tipped his hand to his hat and said:

'Afternoon, old chap. I've just been sent out by the War Office to take over your Battalion.'

'The hell you have,' bellowed Pearson, rising to his feet.

'Terribly sorry, old man,' said Gofton-Salmond. 'Nothing personal, you know. Fortunes of war and all that.'

By now Pearson was standing right in front of Gofton-Salmond, his pipe dancing under the other man's nose.

'Understand this,' said Pearson. 'You are not taking over any battalion around here. This is my Battalion and it is going to stay my Battalion.'

Pearson, a burly, boyish 27-year-old, was apparently considered too young by the War Office, and it had been decided to replace him by an older man. The problem of two commanding officers was further complicated the next day by the return of James Hill.

Hill had trained himself to walk again by leaving the hospital through the French windows of his room by night, unbeknown to the authorities. When he judged himself fit enough, he returned to the 1st Parachute Brigade without medical clearance. The fact that his wounds had to be dressed regularly gave him away. That night there was a discreet move from the bar, by the three colonels, to claim the Commanding Officer's seat at the top of the dinner table. Pearson won. Gofton-Salmond tried manfully to make his presence felt. Hill manoeuvred adroitly to regain control. And Pearson went on being Pearson.

The men put aside their games of pontoon and found something new on which to gamble— the CO Stakes. According to the Battalion diary, Pearson was odds-on favourite, Hill was 5-1 against, and Gofton-Salmond was the 10-1 outsider.

The Battalion Doctor helped Pearson stay in command by obtaining information on Gofton-Salmond. He discovered that he had recently been suffering from piles, and so, using a routine medical as cover, Dr Heggie pronounced him unfit for immediate service, and two days later he was gone. Hill now realized that the only commanding officer the 1st Battalion would accept was Alastair Pearson. This was the result of the remarkable confidence built up between him and the soldiers during the recent heavy fighting. He went and told the Brigade Commander, who shared his views. In order to get Hill out of trouble with the general hospital in Algiers, an irate Brigade Commander had him flown back to the UK. The bookmakers made a clean-up as Hill departed for England. The Adjutant noted:

'Loading tables are far easier when there is only one colonel.'

The struggle for power was over and Pearson was still firmly in command.

Late in January the Battalion again got down to the serious business of war. They had, by then, been moved back to Algiers, from whence on the 25th of the month they sailed to Bone and from there set off on a 300-mile journey by truck. They drove through the precipitous Kabylie mountains to the foothills commanding the Tunis plains, where the Germans had built a string of hilltop strongholds. They arrived near their objective on 30 January.

The German fortifications looked impregnable. The triple peak of Djebel Mansour commanded a deep valley half a mile broad and overlooked the main road to Tunis on the other side. All along the right flank, a massive German build-up threatened the slowly advancing Allied armies. Something was needed to relieve the pressure.

The next day, 31 January, Pearson was ordered to seize and hold Djebel Mansour and Djebel Alliliga on the following night. By attacking the Germans on the Djebels, it was hoped to force them to withdraw their troops from other fronts to deal with the situation.

'All we have to do is irritate them for a day or two,' Pearson told his officers as they surveyed the jagged bluffs of Mansour, where the Germans had established a network of infantry trenches, mortar batteries and machine-gun nests.

A company of French Foreign Legionnaires, dug into a wood in the valley, had been shelling the Germans day after day without making any impression.

'Alas, Colonel,' the French Commander, Capitaine Favreau, told Pearson, 'Mansour can never be taken.'

'Oh, I don't know, we might have a shot at it.'

'It is madness,' said Favreau.

'War is usually mad,' Pearson replied.

The next night, a patrol commanded by Captain Vic Coxen raced to the top of Mansour through withering machine-gun fire and mortar explosions. They sliced through a company of Germans and came back with prisoners, plus detailed plans of the layout of the enemy's position.

Pearson went along to have a look for himself, while leaving the mechanics of the patrol to Coxen. Modern commanders might find this sort of action by the Commanding Officer rather foolhardy, but Pearson realized that it was vital. It was this sort of example that set him apart from other leaders and gave his men the inspiration and determination to succeed against impossible odds.

To assist Pearson's Battalion, there was support in the form of the 3rd Battalion, Grenadier Guards, who were to take over the positions vacated by the 1st Battalion, and a company of the Foreign Legion. Pearson's plan was for R and T Companies to take Djebel Mansour and then move along the ridge and take Alliliga.

The attack, postponed until 0500 hours on 3 February, was launched in the wet darkness of the North African night. As the French artillery barrage lifted, they scrambled up the steep sides of the mountain, leaping and ducking from boulder to bush to avoid the storm of fire that crashed down from the German positions above.

The fusillade tore gaps in the line of advancing paratroopers. One soldier fell, his legs shattered. Two of his mates stopped to help him, but it was obvious that there was nothing that could save him. One of the soldiers pulled a tangerine from his pocket to moisten the dying man's lips. He started to peel it.

'Here, I'll do that myself,' said the wounded man. 'It's my legs I've lost, not my hands!' Calmly he ate his tangerine in the first light of that awful dawn. As he savoured the final segment, he lay back his head and died.

An officer called Captain Turnbull went down too, shot in the body. He waved on the men who stopped to help him.

'Never mind me,' he shouted. 'Get to the top of the mountain first.'

They found him again, two days later, semi-paralysed and grey with hunger, but alive. Another soldier, Paddy Ryan, fell. In his bulging pockets he carried several thousand Francs, won the night before the battle in a game of pontoon. His anxious comrades were keeping a very close watch on Paddy as they fought their way up the mountain. When he fell, two of them sprang forward to help him and his gambling fortune. But Paddy shook them off:

'I'm not dead, yet,' he cried. 'I just tripped up.' He jumped up again and charged on upwards, only to become a prisoner of war, along with his winnings!

S Company was in serious trouble, having gone astray because the white guide tapes had been cut by an enemy patrol. They stumbled through a booby-trapped minefield into the direct fire of the German machine guns, firing on fixed lines. They were caught in a frenzy of explosions and tracer fire.

Among the casualties was one of the bravest young officers in the Battalion, Captain Phillip Mellor. He had already lost an eye in a grenade explosion. He was hurled skywards, his left leg blown off by a mine. As he lay semi-conscious on the exposed mountainside, a burst of fire ripped through his body. But still he lived. Heaving himself on to his elbows, he crawled painfully towards the machine gun, emptied his pistol at the German gunners and died. 'No braver man ever lived.'

Within half an hour the first paratroopers had reached the crest of the mountains. Led by Captain Vic Coxen, the first wave swarmed over the final ridge and charged across the flat top of the mountain into the German trenches. All over the battlefield could be heard the battle cry of the paratroopers: '*Waho Mohammed*'.

One by one the German machine guns were silenced as the paratroopers put them to the bayonet.

Pearson charged up the mountain with his headquarters group. As he rounded a clump of bushes near the summit, he came face to face with two Germans. He whipped out his revolver and squeezed the trigger. Nothing happened. He squeezed again. Again an empty click. He had forgotten to load it. Cursing volubly, he looked up from the pistol to face the Germans and what he thought were his last moments. They were standing whitefaced, with their hands above their heads, captured by the power of Pearson's invective! He threw his revolver aside, handed the prisoners over to his bodyguard, and led the rest of the men on a swing to the right to begin the second phase of the attack – the assault on Djebel Alliliga.

However, by this time the number of paratroopers had thinned considerably and the first impetus of the attack was slowing down. The Germans, recovering from the initial assault, were sending their runaway troops back to counter-attack. They came at the paratroopers on Alliliga with a new ferocity and succeeded in dislodging them from their secondary objective. Pearson took his men back to the captured positions on Mansour and prepared to hang on as long as he could. Barely an hour had passed since the battle had started.

The paratroopers consolidated their positions on Mansour as they occupied the well-prepared German defences. British casualties had been heavy, but German casualties were heavier. Their dead littered the mountain top. On the 1st Battalion's left flank the French Legionnaires had launched an assault on a position known as Point 646, ground of vital importance which overlooked Mansour. The French managed to throw the Germans off the position.

Meanwhile, Pearson was organizing the defence of Djebel Mansour, for he knew that the Germans would put in a counter-attack after bombarding the position. He used abandoned German equipment, turning their mortars and machine guns down the slope to face the Tunis road, along which the Germans were preparing their counter-attack. More and more of their troops poured in, called from other fronts to help deal with the menace on Mansour.

As the day wore on, it became clear that the Allied plan had worked. Pearson watched a squadron of German Stuka dive-bombers take off from the roadway and head for Mansour. All day the Stukas screamed down on the position like angry hornets.

They also dropped into the valley beyond to terrify the Arab muleteers who were driving their teams up the mountain paths, bringing vital reserve ammunition and supplies to the paratroopers. The muleteers panicked and fled, but the situation was saved by Peter Cleasby-Thompson and a French officer, Major Prioleau. They jumped on to horses and grabbed a pair of mules each, leading them up Djebel Mansour.

Most of the day the paratroopers crouched in their trenches, sheltering from the fierce air bombardment. Pearson constantly dashed from trench to trench, reassuring his men, directing their fire and supervising the evacuation of the wounded. It was this inspiring leadership that kept up the soldiers' morale and made them fight back even harder. He was a master at organizing and fighting a battle from a hastily set-up defensive position. He made himself seen by the soldiers, defying death and conducting the battle at the same time. Many might argue that the Commanding Officer should not place his life in jeopardy in such a manner, but I believe that when things begin to get really tough the leader must be seen. Many of his officers had been wounded or killed and Pearson realized that he had to get round his men and rally them.

A German machine gun on Djebel Alliliga was raking a section of Pearson's defence line with paralysing accuracy. The Germans overlooked the British trenches and, any time that they saw movement on Mansour, they perforated the area with shot. Pearson had been on the radio several times to the Grenadier Guards, asking for the removal of this threat. But the Guards had failed in their attack. They had fought valiantly for the mountain all day, bush by bush, rock by rock, but the Germans had thrown them back. And still the machine gun went on firing, making life extremely uncomfortable for those on Djebel Mansour.

For thirty-six hours the paratroopers clung to the top of Mansour, while the Germans sent in wave after wave of troops in their atempts to drive the British off. On the morning of 5 February, just as dawn was breaking, Pearson and his men heard heavy firing coming from the French positions on the left flank. The beleaguered French were overrun and driven back into the valley, their commander fighting every inch of the way, even when he had lost an eye. Their sergeant-major led a spirited bayonet charge in an attempt to retake the position, but overwhelming German forces told him that their situation was hopeless.

The 1st Battalion were now on their own on the mountain. They were overlooked by the Germans on the left, on the right and in front. They were running desperately short of ammunition and the enemy were moving in for the kill.

'Let's see how long we can hang on,' said Pearson, knowing

that, unless reinforcements arrived soon, their position would be untenable.

However, two of his men were not prepared to wait. They were both Scots and, with the ingenuity of true Pearson men, they had found liquor in the middle of the desert and were now the worse for wear.

'I'm no waitin' here to be plugged by you lot,' said the first Scot. 'Let's you and I get oot o' here.'

So he and his mate climbed unsteadily out of their trenches and staggered down the mountain towards the grey flood of advancing German infantry, moving cautiously upwards towards the paratroopers.

'We're going tae capture Von Arnim,' the tipsy Scots shouted to their comrades, who tried to call them back. They ignored their pleas and strode jerkily on, their sub-machine guns blasting from their hips. They were never seen again, but it was later learned that, miraculously, they had survived to become prisoners.

By 0915 hours that morning the Battalion's mortars had run out of ammunition. The German artillery barrage was total. The only men who moved were dead men, thrown up by the explosions. Those who still lived burrowed deeper into their trenches to escape the bombardment. And all the time the German infantry climbed steadily on up the mountain.

By 1000 hours, S Company was left only with grenades, and R and T Companies had about a hundred rounds between them – most of which was with T Company. Suddenly the shelling stopped. Silently the paratroopers waited for the Germans to attack. Pearson had radioed for permission to withdraw and save what was left of his Battalion, but permission did not come. So he told his men to hold their ground 'Come what may.'

He went to the edge of the ridge and stood there watching the advancing enemy, judging their strength, calculating where their forward troops would strike first. Shots were whining around him, but he stood his ground as he always did, protected only by the conviction that they would not get him. Other officers were not so fortunate. One major raised himself above his trench to see where the Germans were and fell immediately, a bullet between his eyes.

The first tentative German assault was thrown back. S Company, now out of ammunition, collected piles of rocks with which to fight off the next attack. Pearson knew that the time had come to pull out. He radioed Brigade Headquarters again, asking permission to withdraw.

'You'll get a decision in ten minutes,' he was told.

'Ten minutes will be too bloody late!' he roared back into the mouthpiece.

The Germans rushed forward and dropped to the ground only forty yards from the British positions.

'Good morning, Tommy,' they shouted. 'What regiment are you?' And with their greeting, they sent a cascade of rifle fire, grenades and mortar bombs.

The paratroopers shouted back:

'Come a little closer, Hermann. We're just having a brew up.'

Then they slung their rocks, the few remaining grenades, even empty magazines. They fixed their bayonets, ready for the final onslaught.

Pearson was on the radio again and was told to wait five minutes.

'Five minutes will be too late. Another two minutes and there will be no one here to answer the radio!' He was given permission to withdraw. He crashed down the mouthpiece and yelled: 'Withdraw.'

A section of riflemen, using the last of T Company's ammunition, formed an arc on the top of the mountain to protect the rest of the Battalion as they carefully backed over the ridge. They stumbled down into the valley, limping and falling, most of them wounded, many on blood-soaked stretchers. The paratroopers wound their way down the mountain paths under constant shelling from the pursuing Germans. But the men were so exhausted that they barely had the energy to get out of the way of the blasts. At last they found the safety of the Allied lines under the trees.

Few men had ever been subjected to such a ferocious

attack. For a day and a half, most of the time without food or rest, they had faced the kind of punishment that should have annihilated them several times over. Although they had finally given up, their action had served its purpose in relieving pressure on the Allied Front.

Some days later Lieutenant-Colonel Alastair Pearson was decorated in the field with a DSO. After the brief ceremony, he gathered his men around him to make a speech— something he seldom did. He wanted to clear up a few points for the fresh-faced youths who had been sent up from Algiers to replace the Battalion's casualties on Mansour— thirteen officers killed and wounded, and one hundred and sixty-nine other ranks killed, wounded or missing.

He pushed his hand through his woolly hair, cleared his throat and said in his gruff Scottish voice, 'I just want to tell you men that you have joined the finest fighting Battalion in this war. And this DSO doesn't belong to me. It belongs to all the men who were on Mansour. We didn't beat the Germans on Mansour, as you all know. We bloody well thrashed them!'

A veteran paratrooper turned to a new recruit and said, 'That's the man we call 'Mad Jock'!'

Pearson had shown that he had the ability to command a battalion in war. Despite his antipathy towards the more senior officers back at headquarters, he nevertheless obeyed his orders to the letter. He could have withdrawn from Djebel Mansour at an earlier stage in the battle, claiming that the wireless had been blown up. However, he not only stayed in position but demanded that his soldiers did likewise. It was the sheer force of his personality that inspired the men of the 1st Battalion to hold on until the very last minute.

VI

Tamera

After the battle for Djebel Mansour the 1st Battalion stayed in the area around Bou Arada. Here they sorted themselves out, took on reinforcements from the Royal Welch Fusiliers and generally prepared for the next assignment. They remained in the area with the rest of the 1st Parachute Brigade for about three weeks.

The whole brigade front was subject to sporadic attacks from time to time, which caused a few casualties. However, on 26 February, 1943, the Germans decided to put in a concentrated attack. Pearson possessed an uncanny sixth sense as to when and where the enemy were going to attack and had prepared his defences accordingly.

It had been a day of vicious and bloody fighting during which the Germans and Italians had repeatedly tried to break up the British front with terrifying artillery barrages, followed up by suicidal infantry charges against the British wire. All their efforts had failed and now, as the end of the day drew near, four hundred dead and wounded Germans and Italians litterd the battlefield. By some telepathic mutual consent both sides seemed to have agreed it was time to rest and recover the wounded.

But Pearson had one more task for his men before they opened their tins of bully beef and gnawed their hardtack biscuits.

'Tell the boys to dig in,' he ordered his company commanders.

The order was received with a universal groan. No soldier likes digging trenches, and paratroopers least of all. They objected to digging trenches, especially when the sun was going down and it appeared obvious that the fighting was over for the day.

'Old Jock's gone crazy,' they told each other, as they scratched the rocky earth with their shovels. 'He must have hit his head today.'

Pearson listened to their groans as he swept through the lines shouting encouragement, clouds of smoke belching from his greasy black pipe.

'Any man who doesn't dig a deep enough trench will be forced to eat two cans of bully beef instead of one!' he threatened.

By the time the black North African night had fallen, the trenches were finished. Pearson seemed pleased.

'Very nice,' he said. 'Now let's pack up all our kit and get the hell out of here.'

The men were aghast.

'That's it,' they said. 'He's finally cracked. Mad Jock has gone mad at last.'

Cajoled and bullied by their officers, they strapped on their packs and ammunition belts again. Picking up their weapons, they moved off into the darkness, Pearson at the front, leading them.

A short distance away, he stopped the Battalion.

'Now, gentlemen,' he said, 'You may eat.'

Baffled and angry, his men once again tackled the near impossible task of trying to make themselves comfortable. An hour later, just as the games of cards had started under the groundsheets, the night was blasted by German mortar fire. Machine-guns traced murderous cross-fire over the hillside. All the fire was directed at the empty slit trenches, so reluctantly dug by Pearson's men.

Watching the fireworks from the safety of their new position, Pearson alerted his men for action.

'I think we can expect a visit fairly soon,' he said. 'We must prepare a welcome for our friends.'

The paratroopers spread out along the flank of the bombarded slit trenches and waited for the barrage to stop. When it did, a shadowy swarm of German infantrymen swooped on the empty trenches. They found nothing to attack and wandered around in confusion. Their bewilderment was complete when Pearson and his men fell on them, scything through their lines like a deadly desert storm. The first blow knocked all the fight out of the Germans. Those who survived surrendered immediately.

This uncanny instinct was to come to Pearson's aid many times during the war. In battle after battle he was to show a natural genius for outwitting the enemy and inflicting maximum damage, with the minimum losses to his own troops. His stamina was prodigious. He rarely slept. He could live for days off a can of sardines. Although he was a tough commander, he also showed a great generosity of spirit and warm concern for the men who served under him.

One man went to his tent to ask for an advance of his meagre pay to send home to his wife and child, both of whom were sick and in urgent need of funds.

'The Army will take too long to send it,' said Pearson. 'How much to you want?' He signed his own cheque and handed it over to the soldier.

Another soldier walked into the middle of a circle of officers whom Pearson was briefing one day. The soldier laid down his rifle and said quietly:

'I'll have to pack it in, Sir. I can't fight any more.'

Pearson put him under immediate arrest. But before he could decide what to do with him, the Battalion was sent back into action. The soldier who would no longer fight was sent with the medical unit to establish a First Aid Post in a cave. The cave was hit by a shell and everyone in it was killed. When Pearson came to the arrested man's papers, he stamped across them, 'Killed In Action'.

'We don't want to shame his people,' he said. 'He wasn't a coward. It took a brave man to come to me and lay down his rifle.'

Yet a sergeant-major who stole the rum ration was court-martialled and sent home in disgrace.

'I can understand an honest doubt of conscience,' said Pearson. 'But I cannot stomach a man who'll use his position to take advantage of soldiers fighting in a war.'

Although the paratroopers fought with honour, a barbaric

and gruesome war was being waged on their flank. Arabs captured and butchered soldiers from both sides, to loot their bodies. The Moroccan Goums, with whom the paratroopers had often fought, sold their prisoners to their French officers or to the Americans, and produced ears to support their claims of kills. They were not fussy about where the ears came from. Once, when Pearson sent a young officer to collect some German prisoners from a Goum encampment, the officer returned alone to report grimly: 'All the prisoners died in the night.'

Yet there was a degree of respect, something almost approaching affection, between the German and the British paratroopers. The Germans had quickly recognized the superior fighting ability of the paratroopers, had christened them 'The Red Devils' and had issued special instructions detailing the best methods to use when fighting them.

The 1st Parachute Brigade handed over the Bou Arada sector to the Americans on 5 March, 1943, and moved to the valley of Tamera. The Germans were hemmed in on the coastal plains around Tunis by the steel ring of the massive Allied forces; frantically, they sought a way out. General von Arnim thought he had found an escape route along a coast road which ran from Tamera to Algiers.

Pearson's men dug into the steep sides of the lower slopes of the scrub-covered hills just outside the village of Tamera. It was tough fighting country. The prickly cactus bushes grew waist high and the paratroopers were forced to lie on beds of razor-sharp needles. The alternative battleground was a thick wood of cork trees along the summit of the hill which would have been impossible to defend.

As the drizzling dawn broke on the morning of 8 March the waiting paratroopers saw the first German troops emerging from the mists on the road winding along the valley floor. Slowly the grey column grew longer and longer, snaking forward like a great worm. The Germans marched calmly and precisely in formation, apparently unaware that they were being overlooked from the ridge above them.

The mortar and machine-gun crews fixed their sights on

the advancing men. Silently they brought their rifles and Bren guns to bear on the marching columns, their hand grenades lying in neat piles beside them. The paratroopers were accustomed to exercising patience in such a situation. Pearson never gave the order to fire until the last possible moment, and he demanded complete silence before such an attack. His men knew what it was to run out of ammunition and every man was trained to make all his shots count.

He stood quietly in the bushes, watching the advancing foe. Then, when the road was filled with Germans only three hundred yards away, he turned to his radio operator and said:

'Tell the gunners to get busy.'

From behind the 1st Battalion's position, a battery of 25-pounder field guns ranged on the road and raked it with shellfire. The ridge exploded with fire from the hidden paratroopers and the Germans disappeared in a cloud of dust. Scores of them fell and lay still, and the survivors scattered into the woods and ditches on the other side of the road. The valley of Tamera was filled with hideous echoes that were not to die away for five days.

The Germans' mortars and guns were giving S Company, under the command of Major Lloyd-Jones, an unpleasant time with some accurate fire. Pearson visited S Company and decided to send T Company out on a sweep to clear away the enemy. They returned some three hours later with about a hundred prisoners, a mixture of Alpine 30 (Marsch Battalion) and Witzig's Parachute Engineers. They also captured three infantry guns and much equipment.

The German forces in the Tamera sector included the Barenthin Regiment, which had among its ranks a number of Luftwaffe men. There was also the Tunisian Regiment, which was made up of German reserves in the Mediterranean theatre; the 10th Panzer Grenadier Regiment and the Witzig Regiment of Parachute Engineers. The latter troops were highly trained and had taken part in the raid on the Belgian fortress of Eben Emael.

On that first day the British and Germans were locked in

a nightmare struggle in which it was frequently impossible to distinguish friend from foe. All over the side of the hill grim little battles were being fought in the mist and smoke. Bayonets thudded home as men dashed through the bushes seeking targets. As the day wore on the mist cleared and the blazing sun burned down on a scene of horror. Bodies lay grotesquely behind boulders, propped up in bushes, sprawled in slit trenches, covered with the macabre black dust thrown up by exploding mortar bombs.

The Germans were still pouring troops into the battle as Pearson led his men down the valley, slicing through the German reinforcements. Repeatedly he sent his platoons sweeping in wide paths through the enemy lines, while others in the 1st Battalion's area mopped up the Germans trapped inside. By keeping the ground in front of his positions clear, he cut the German attackers in two and prevented them from overpowering the paratroopers by sheer weight of numbers.

Late in the afternoon the situation became critical again. The forward company, S Company, was being overrun on the lower slopes and the Germans began a bloody massacre. Major Lloyd-Jones and Lieutenant Cairne were reported wounded; Lieutenant Sinclair had been killed and Lieutenant Norton, who had stayed with S Company's mortar detachment, had also been killed.

Pearson ordered T Company, who were standing by, to counterattack. At 1700 hours the position was retaken, Captain Stephenson dying in the assault. By 1800 hours the situation was under control once more and a report to this effect was sent back to Brigade. At the end of the first day the paratroopers were badly battered but they had not lost an inch of ground. When darkness fell and the sound of firing had died down, Pearson went round his companies to count the cost and consolidate his resources.

He had lost five officers and nearly one hundred men, but they had taken two hundred prisoners and the ridge which they defended was littered with many more dead Germans. Pearson noted in the Battalion diary:

'It has been a hot sunny day and the Bn was glad when the evening came.'

'We're rather thin on the ground, Sir,' said Major Hall.

'So are the Germans,' replied Pearson, pointing over the darkened battlefield to where little groups of medical staff from both sides were searching for wounded.

In their trenches the paratroopers tried to rest and discovered a curious new-found affinity for their fellow men. Strangely, the carnage brought out the best in them. The meanest man in the Battalion would halve his last cigarette with his worst enemy. The division of rank between officers and men disappeared and even the most detested sergeant suddenly became a warm friend. In the face of death the paratroopers developed a deeply sensitive awareness of life and savoured every moment. Some inner determination drove them to rescue the wounded who lay bleeding and groaning in No-Man's-Land. It seemed vitally important to save the faintest spark of life, even if the life was that of an enemy.

As he looked over the battlefield, Pearson saw two Scotsmen, Sergeant Jock Rainnie from Aberdeen and Private Jock McCutcheon, bringing in a wounded man. It was Lieutenant Cairne, one of the men cut down in Major Taffy Lloyd-Jones's company. Cairne was dying but he insisted on telling his rescuers that out in the darkness lay another man waiting to be saved.

'I've been lying out there for hours listening to him tapping two stones together to attract attention,' said Cairne. 'You must try and bring him in.'

Cairne was taken back to the First Aid Post and Rainnie and McCutcheon went out once more into No-Man's-Land to search for be the wounded man. Although it was nearly daylight and they were in danger of being caught in the open when the battle resumed, they hunted until they found him. He was a young German. The two Scots lifted him between them and carried him back to their lines. Pearson bent over the wounded man:

'The war's over for you, my lad,' he said. 'We'll look after you.'

The German smiled thinly:

'You are Scottish?'

'Yes,' Sergeant Rainnie told him.

'I studied at Glasgow University for many years,' said the German. 'The Scots are a wonderful people. I admire your poets. Do you know:

> My heart's in the Highlands
> My heart is not here
> My heart's in the Highlands
> A chasing the deer . . . ?'

The three Scotsmen were silent. Tears streamed down the German's face. 'I wish to thank you for saving my life,' he said.

Sergeant Rainnie was the first to speak. 'It makes you wonder what the blody war is all about,' he said gruffly.

'Take the boy away and get him fixed up,' said Pearson.

Within the hour the battle blazed once more into life. All day mortar duels pock-marked the hills, explosions scooping holes in the lines of trenches. But the Germans made no frontal attack. Pearson sent out fighting patrols through the woods and gullies to bring back stray Germans. Lieutenant Mayhew attacked an enemy company in a nearby Arab village where he captured twelve prisoners and killed thirteen others without loss to his own party.

A troop of five Churchill tanks clattered noisily through the paratrooper's lines with the determination of a team of referees come to settle an argument, but only one returned about an hour later. About mid-afternoon a German ambulance drove along the road under the noses of Pearson's men and pulled up under the trees on the other side of the valley. The back door opened and a steel-helmeted mortar squad jumped out, but before they had a chance to use their weapon they had been cut down by rifle fire. So it went on all the second day, with the Germans pushing forward on all flanks.

The next day, 10 March, the Germans opened up with a very heavy mortar bombardment on the 1st and 2nd Battalion's positions. These bombardments were followed up by infantry attacks. T Company was overrun and Pearson led a party of cooks and clerks in the counter-attack. The position was recaptured, but Pearson had insufficient troops to man all the forward positions and he had to hold a smaller perimeter which was overlooked by the Germans on Djebel Bel. The 2nd Battalion had also been attacked but had managed to hang on to their positions, though they were unable to stop the enemy from cutting the two battalions off from each other.

One of Pearson's sections took an entire salvo which killed most of them. Private Donald Wigley, a brawny young lad from Yorkshire, fearfully raised his head from his trench. Barney Ross, a tough little Scot who liked to play the mouth organ, lay crushed. Nobby Clarke from Aberdeen was dead also, although there was not a mark on him. Neil Johnston lay still, his body shattered. A man called Burns had lost a leg and died while Wigley watched, helpless.

Wigley scrambled from his trench and half-fell down the hill to a trench where a soldier called Smudger Smith, from Greenock, lay badly wounded. He pulled Smith out and carried him up the slope away from the trenches.

As he dressed Smith's wounds, the mortars started up again and a bomb exploded only a few yards away. Shrapnel tore into Wigley's back, but he was still able to get to his feet. He turned round to get Smith, but he was dead. Despite his wounds, Wigley went on to help another soldier called Ferguson, from Edinburgh, who had lost a leg. There was little Wigley could do as the position was exposed to the Germans and there were no medical staff about. He set up his Bren gun facing down the hill towards the advancing Germans.

'Don't worry,' he told Ferguson. 'We'll soon be out of here.'

Suddenly the two men were surrounded by a German patrol which came on them from behind. Wigley reached for his Bren gun but the German officer kicked it away.

'This is very bad,' he said. 'Your friend is badly wounded.'

The Germans did what they could for Ferguson and left him with a bottle of water as they marched Wigley away. A

few minutes later Ferguson died. Wigley was taken to the
German lines only a hundred and fifty yards away.

On 12 March Lieutenant-General C. W. Allfrey, the Corps
Commander, visited the Parachute Brigade and to his surprise found the paratroopers 'in great heart', despite the
continual German bombardment. Allfrey decided that, in
spite of the lack of troops, the Djebel Bel had to be captured
if the paratroopers were to remain in their present positions.
The 1st Battalion were all around the base of the hill and
their every move could be observed by the Germans on the
top. That day the Sherwood Foresters made a valiant attempt
to capture the hill and very nearly succeeded, but were
beaten off the top by a vigorous German charge.

By the evening of 12 March the paratroopers were fighting
by instinct alone. Without sleep, without food and with little
water, they fought fiercely on and still somehow kept the
Germans at bay. There were twins in the Battalion, Tony
and Teddy Barker, from London. During a lull in the
fighting, Tony confided his fears to Jock Rainnie:

'By all the laws of average,' he said, 'one of us is bound to
be knocked out. They can't keep slinging this stuff at us
without one of us copping it.' Before the day was over both
were to die.

At his headquarters in the middle of the Battalion position,
Pearson took a radio message from Allfrey. It read:

'I call upon every man to stand his ground. Fight to the
last. There must be no question of a withdrawal of any size
without a definite order, so that we have a firm base from
which to hit them back.'

Pearson handed the message to his new Adjutant, Chris
Perrin-Brown.

'It looks as if we've got to fight off the whole bloody
German Army again,' he said. 'I don't know what they'd do
without us.'

He had only one officer left for each company, his men
were drawn into a tight perimeter, completely overlooked by
the enemy on the upper heights. A rattle of small-arms fire
spattered around his position. He looked up to see forty or

more grey-smocked German paratroopers rushing up the hill towards his headquarters, forcing before them the remnants of a company of Sherwood Foresters who had come to relieve the 1st Battalion. Pearson whipped out his pistol from its holster and shouted: 'It's Witzig's men. Let's go and get the bastards!'

His clerks and signallers grabbed their guns. Engineers, drivers, messengers, batmen and cooks scrambled frantically for their little-used rifles. A rifle was thrust into the hands of Brigadier Eric Down, who happened to be visiting the Battalion at the time. Shouting some unintelligible ancestral war cry, Pearson descended on the Germans at the head of this last-ditch throng, laying about him with an aweful exuberance. The Germans hesitated before the screaming mob charging down on them, spouting a hurricane of bullets and grenades, then turned tail and fled. Their retreat turned into a general rout which infected stronger German forces coming round the bottom of the hill to consolidate what they thought was a breakthrough.

The fleeing Germans ran straight across the killing area of Pearson's entrenched company crackshots and were gunned down almost to a man. At the height of the fight Sergeant Jock Rainnie and a detachment arrived at Battalion Head-quarters from their own position. They had been sent by a worried subaltern to 'help out the old man'. As they ran forward, Lance-Corporal Coster, one of Pearson's bodguards, waved them back.

'Get down,' he shouted.

Then he pulled the pin out of a grenade and lobbed it into a bush about thirty yards away from Battalion Headquarters. It exploded on landing, killing the two Germans who had been in the bush.

'The cheeky beggars were waiting to knock off 'Mad Jock' when he got back,' said Coster. The Germans made no more attempts to overrun what was left of the 1st Battalion and their encirclement was broken.

That same evening the 1st Battalion was moved out of the line for a well-deserved rest. After a two-day rest by the sea and strengthened by reinforcements, the Battalion was ordered back into the line in the hills. The Germans were making a determined effort to break through and seize the vital Tunisian coastal road.

The key position was a hill called Sidi Bou Dalla, otherwise known as Bowler Hat. A battalion of the Leicester Regiment had been thrown off Bowler Hat and the Germans were using it as an observation post, from which they directed their deadly artillery barrages. The Leicesters were relieved by the 3rd Parachute Battalion, who were also ordered to take Bowler Hat. Their commander had little time to make a decent reconnaissance and the subsequent attack failed. It was now the 1st Battalion's turn.

General Allfrey had sent for Pearson and said, 'That hill has got to be taken.'

'Not by me, Sir,' said Pearson. 'I'm too tired and my men are even more tired.'

The General was not amused. But Pearson was no respector of high-ranking officers. He was prepared to risk his command to protect his men. To him it was a highly dangerous, even suicidal mission. He estimated that an attack on Bowler Hat would cost him a hundred men.

After what he later described as 'a bit of an argy bargy with the General', he returned to his men with a compromise. He would take the hill if his men did not have to face the hazardous task of defending it against German counter-attacks. Allfrey had promised to relieve the Battalion as soon as they had captured Bowler Hat.

The mission was still no picnic. Lieutenant-Colonel Johnny Frost, Pearson's old friend who commanded the 2nd Battalion, told him, 'You've bitten off more than you can chew this time, Alastair.' As they shook hands, Frost had the real fear that he was saying goodbye to Pearson for the last time.

Pearson went in the next night, 23 March, at 2230 hours. Silently he led his men round the back of the hill in the dark and swooped on the Germans as they slept. The Panzer Grenadiers who had been holding the hill had just been relieved, and the German infantry who had replaced them had not settled in. Only fifteen rounds of ammunition were fired and Pearson did not lose a man. One German was killed and about forty prisoners were taken. The attack itself was brilliant and it remains today a classic example of a battalion night attack.

Some hours later, in the German rear positions, Pearson supervised the mopping-up operations. He had captured maps showing German defence plans around Bizerta. One man leaned in a trench wearing a German helmet. Pearson turned to Jock Clements, one of his bodyguards, and said, 'Tell that bloody fool to take off that helmet before someone shoots him by mistake.'

Clements went over to the man and swung him round.

'But he IS German, Sir!' he shouted.

They found four more Germans sleeping under a tarpaulin in the trench— they had slept through the whole attack!

As daybreak came Pearson took a few men and went forward to probe the German lines. During their approach they ran into an ambush as they crossed an exposed piece of ground. The Germans caught sight of them and opened up with mortar bombs. The paratroopers flattened themselves against the hard rubble of the desert.

'Don't move,' bellowed Pearson. 'Wait till they stop.'

It was to be two hours before the bombing stopped, and for two hours the sweating, frightened men waited for Pearson's order to run for it. The order never came. The only thing he said was, 'I wish to God I had a drink.'

When it was all over, the ashen paratroopers crawled back to safety, shaken and bruised, but still alive. They arrived back on Bowler Hat in time to be dive-bombed by twenty Stukas. A squadron of Spitfires came to their rescue and put paid to nine of the enemy planes. A little later the 3rd Parachute Battalion took over the position, allowing the 1st and 2nd Parachute Battalions to prepare for the final offensive against the Germans.

First Army had been reinforced and moved up to join the Eighth Army. Both armies were under the command of General Alexander. Opposing them was the Axis army of some three hundred thousand men commanded by von Arnim. Rommel had by now returned to Germany, leaving behind his famous Afrika Korps. The task given to the 1st Parachute Brigade was to destroy the enemy that threatened the coastal road. The Brigade Commander, Brigadier Flavell's task was to free the main road axis and, to assist him in this difficult job, he was given the artillery of the 46th Infantry Division.

On 27 March the great advance began. The Allies bulldozed forward over the baking plains, guns booming away in support, tanks grinding and clanking forwards, with wave after wave of dust-covered, red-faced troops battling steadily onwards. The whole advance covered a front of a hundred miles from north to south as they pressed on towards Tunis and Bizerta.

On the northern front, 1st Parachute Brigade, supported on the left by units of Moroccan Goums and the Foreign Legion, fought again over the green battleground of Tamera, where earlier that month they had lost so many men.

Pearson's objective was a great rock-strewn bowl surrounded by jagged ridges, where Italian and German troops had dug in to make a final stand. He recruited a local Arab to lead the battalion through the wild, muddy valleys and the bewildering cork forests which lay in their path. He took a 1000 Franc note from his pocket, tore it in half and handed one to the Arab.

'You'll get the other half when we get to our destination,' he told the guide.

For fourteen hours, in drenching rain, the paratroopers force-marched across the stony wastes, fording rivers, leaping ditches and using railway tracks to guide them. But as they neared their objective, the first Allied barrage blasted the desert just in front of their advance and the terrified Arab bolted.

Luck, however, was with Pearson, for as his men squelched blindly forward he spotted the glinting dome of a Muslim mosque which was the key to the target. Beyond the mosque lay the great valley leading to the bowl. The paratroopers occupied the bowl with very little difficulty and outflanked both the German and Italian positions. Their attack had hit at the most vulnerable point of the Axis front where the Italian and German lines met. Already the Italians were trudging in to become prisoners.

In the middle of the bowl sat a farm. Pearson ordered a young subaltern, Barney Glick, to take it. With perfect precision, Glick led his platoon in a text-book attack. In the farm he found a despondent Italian colonel, the commander of the elite Bersaglieri Regiment. The colonel handed over his sword in defeat, but refused to be parted from his little pet dog. Soon the 1st Battalion had captured the whole regiment. The barren, ugly hills fluttered with little clouds of white as the Italians swarmed down the valleys clutching handkerchiefs, underwear and white rags in surrender.

The paratroopers took over six hundred prisoners and sent them back behind the lines. The infuriated Germans watched the débâcle from the heights and ordered fighter planes to attack their defeated allies. The Italians probably lost more men to the furious machine-gunning of the German fighters than they did to the British.

The bowl was rapidly becoming a dangerous trap for Pearson's men and he turned them up the ridges to face the tougher German Parachute Engineers, led by his old adversary, Colonel Witzig.

A fierce battle was being fought on a ridge on the right flank where Frost's 2nd Battalion was fighting off heavy counterattacks from two of Witzig's battalions. Forcing their way through the close-packed cork trees in which the Germans had laid rearguard ambushes, Pearson and his men broke through to join Frost and his troops. Several times the Germans nearly pushed them off the ridge as the battle continued. Both sides seemed to know that this was the final showdown. One or other would finally be broken.

Late in the afternoon the battle-weary Germans began to weaken. Pearson's radio operator and three other soldiers pounced on two German machine-gun nests and took them without a fight. He later told Pearson 'The Germans were too nervous to fight. We came up behind them so fast that they didn't know if we were coming or going!'

The battle became a rout and within forty-eight hours the paratroopers had taken all the objectives of two infantry brigades which had been bogged down in the rear. They took another three hundred prisoners, captured eight guns and tons of German supplies. All along the front the story was the same as the Allies forged onwards to victory. The struggle for North Africa was nearly at an end.

The Germans withdrew twenty-four miles back towards Bizerta and the paratroopers lost all contact with them. An American division, the 9th, was sent up to continue the pursuit and tidy up the loose ends. The paratroopers were ordered to break off the fight.

The long ninety days of almost continuous battle were over. It had been a brutal, savage bloodbath, but the paratroopers had paid a fearful price for victory. The Brigade had lost 1,700 men, either killed, wounded or missing. Against this figure they had killed or wounded about 5,000 enemy and taken some 3,600 prisoners.

Week after week, Pearson had crossed off the names of his dwindling Battalion of men and officers killed in action: 'Mellor . . . Wandless . . . Stewart . . . Lloyd-Davies . . . Sinclair . . . Stevenson . . . Hall . . . Wharrier . . . Foggarty . . . Conron . . . Gallagher.'

The survivors were ragged, tired, hungry and sick of the slaughter. But at the same time they were the proudest fighting men in North Africa. The campaign was the first action they had seen and the Brigade had won more medals than any other formation in the British Army: eight Distinguished Service Orders; fifteen Military Crosses; nine Distinguished Conduct Medals; twenty-two Military Medals; three Croix de Guerre and one Legion D'Honneur.

The 1st Battalion had won three DSOs, five MCs, two DCMs and eight MMs. Pearson himself had two DSOs and an MC pinned on his chest.

However, the paratroopers were not thinking of 'gongs' as they climbed aboard the train that was to take them back to the civilised comforts of Algiers. They were thinking of enormous jugs of beer, long cool baths and wild nights in the bistros where they could let off steam.

As the long troop train curved past the barbed wire of the German prisoner-of-war camps, the Germans crowded to the fences to see the victors depart. A low roar came from the thousands of Germans lining the track: '*Rote Teufel, Rote Teufel, Rote Teufel.*'* It broke into a great guttral cheer. The paratroopers stood at the windows of the train and beamed. Some gave the V sign, others raised their hands in a boxer's salute. Alastair Pearson grinned and doffed his red beret. His untidy mop of black hair sprang up at all angles and fell over his face. Behind him his batman fumed.

'Colonel Pearson, Sir,' he said. 'You are a shambles. The first thing you do when you get off this train is have a haircut!'

* Red Devil.

VII

Sicily

Following the completion of the North Africa campaign, the men of the 1st Parachute Brigade set about training and preparing for the invasion of Sicily. A new Brigade Commander had taken over called Gerald Lathbury, (later General Sir Gerald), who had originally commanded the 3rd Parachute Battalion. He sensibly allowed the battalions to train at a relaxed pace as all three had, until recently, been involved in very heavy fighting. Gradually, the pace and pressure of training increased and the paratroopers were once again fit and hard, ready for any fight that lay ahead of them.

The Brigade was training in a desolate valley inaptly named Mascara, in west Algeria, where they were close to their aircraft. The aircraft were American Dakotas, crewed by pilots from 51 US Wing. The paratroopers and the pilots soon got along well, but the British had little confidence in the pilots' navigational abilities. These fears were later to be justified during the assault on Sicily. The Americans had only one navigator to five aircraft and so they flew in a V formation, following the leading aircraft. If the leading aircraft got lost or shot down, then the rest of the group had major problems.

The whole of the 1st Airborne Division moved from the area of Mascara to the vicinity of Kairouan, west of Sousse back in Tunisia. This was accomplished by road, rail and air between 19 June and 5 July, 1943. At the airborne base near Sousse and Kairouan, 51 US Wing and 38 RAF Wing shared six airfields in a wide area of desert. These airfields were little more than dusty strips with no hangars or accommodation. Soldiers and pilots alike were all in tents scattered around the airfields. The troops were able to find some shade by camping in the olive groves nearby. There were also regular trips to the sea, which was only half an hour away by truck from Sousse.

By now the plans were complete. The maps and models were available for the battalion commanders to study and make their detailed plans. The whole operation was code-named 'FUSTIAN', which included the seizing of certain objectives by airborne troops. These troops were to be inserted ahead of General Montgomery's advancing Eighth Army. 13 Corps were due to assault the south-eastern coast of Sicily and move northwards as soon as possible. They had to capture the ports of Syracuse and Augusta quickly, so as to allow their supplies and equipment to be brought in by sea at once. An additional problem, foreseen by the planning staff at General Alexander's Headquarters, was the possibility of strong enemy opposition on the line of the River Simeto, guarding vital airfields not far to the north, near Catania.

The route for Montgomery's advancing 8th Army was to be north-east along the coast road. On this route there were three important bridges to be captured. The first, the Ponte Grande, was captured by a platoon of the 2nd Battalion the South Staffordshire Regiment on the night of 9/10 July, 1943. The second was the Ponte Dei Malati near Lentinia, and this was the task of Number 3 Commando. The third was an ugly girder bridge, the Primosole Bridge. If these three bridges could be taken, then Montgomery's troops would be able to press on and capture Messina, thus cutting off the Germans' line of retreat to mainland Italy.

The Primosole Bridge became the task for the 1st Parachute Brigade and was code-named 'MARSTON'. The plan for the Brigade was that Pearson's 1st Battalion should capture the bridge itself, while Frost's 2nd Battalion held the approaches to the south and E. C. Yeldhams's 3rd Battalion was to hold the northern approaches. It was expected that the leading troops of 13 Corps would make contact with the paratroopers the following morning after their drop. This was important as British intelligence reports predicted considerable enemy opposition, and German, as well as Italian, units were known to be in the area, including armour.

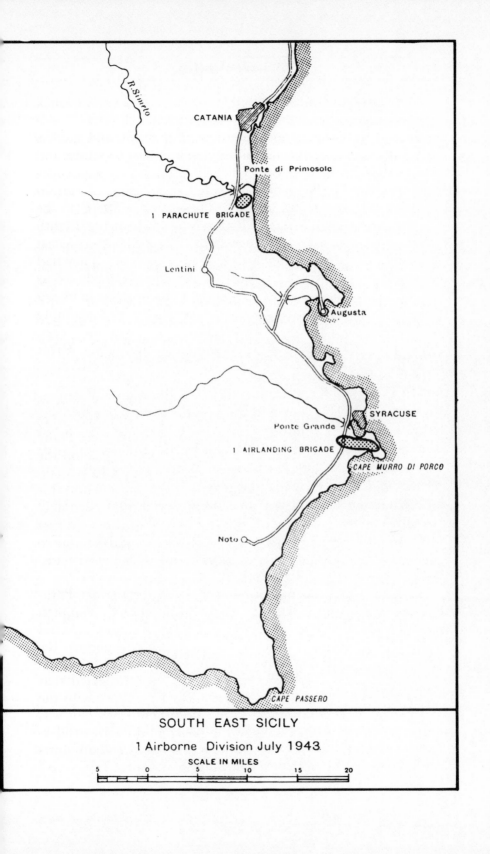

R.Simrto

CATANIA

Ponte di Primosole

1 PARACHUTE BRIGADE

Lentini

Augusta

SYRACUSE

Ponte Grande

1 AIRLANDING BRIGADE

CAPE MURRO DI PORCO

Noto

CAPE PASSERO

SOUTH EAST SICILY

1 Airborne Division July 1943.

SCALE IN MILES

5   0   5   10   15   20

The operation was postponed twenty-four hours, from 12 to 13 July. The confirming order came through to the airborne base during the afternoon of the 13th and the first aircraft took off at 1901 hours that evening. There was a tense and nervous expectancy amongst the paratroopers as they flew one hundred feet above the sea.

Pearson was asleep for most of the trip and was only awakened when his aircraft suddenly lurched upwards, trying to avoid some flak. Outside the aircraft Pearson could see great blobs of fire blazing in the vineyards and fields below. These, he later found out, were haystacks fired by the Germans. His pilot thought they were the wrecks of crashed Dakotas and began to panic. As the first explosive puffs crept towards his plane, the white-faced pilot turned the aircraft round in a tight wheel and sped back to the coast and the safety of the open sea.

In the back of the Dakota Pearson stood up and took off his parachute. He squeezed through the narrow doorway into the cockpit and confronted the two pilots. The co-pilot sat sobbing, his head between his hands. The pilot stared blindly over the sea, willing his plane to safety. The ruddy face of Pearson deepened by several shades.

'What the hell do you two think you're playing at?' he roared.

The pilot clenched his teeth: 'I'm not prepared to go in,' he said. A large and terrible oath drowned the noise of the engines.

'And I,' bellowed Pearson, 'am not prepared to go back.'

The pilot looked nervously over his shoulder at the black-faced warrior fuming down his neck. 'You'll have to go back, Mac,' he said. 'I'm not committing suicide.'

Pearson then took out his revolver and pointed it at the sobbing co-pilot.

'Well, I'd better start off by shooting you, then perhaps it will encourage him,' he said, referring to the pilot. 'And I'll shoot you too, if necessary, because I've got a perfectly good pilot sitting in the back.' The pilot Pearson referred to was an ex-RAF pilot who had been court-martialled several years before for dangerous flying.

The pilot looked into Pearson's eyes and saw that he meant every word, so he agreed to go in, albeit with extreme reluctance. Pearson returned to the cabin, put his parachute back on and waited for the green light that would signal the order to jump.

With the glare of the flares and exploding flak lighting the inside of the aircraft with a red glow, the paratroopers methodically went through their drills as they waited to jump. They checked each others' equipment and signalled that all was in order. Some even found time to smear their hand and faces with anti-mosquito cream as they hooked their static lines to the dropping cable.

The green light flashed on as the plane dived low over the dropping zone. Through the open door Pearson could see the great loop of the River Simeto and their target, the Primosole Bridge, which carried the vital coastal road that went around Sicily. The warm air from the slipstream buffeted his face and his heart began to race as he pushed off out of the door. He tumbled forward and fell like a stone.

Enemy machine-gunners on the ground raked the falling paratroopers with tracer as they fell helplessly to earth. Many were dead by the time they hit the ground. The last man in Pearson's stick was killed because the Dakota was too low by the time he jumped. It was common practice for the Dakota to dive towards the ground, thus raising its tail out of the way of exiting parachutists. This time the pilot had misjudged his height and the consequences were fatal. Those who survived the drop were winded and bruised, but they picked themselves up and made their way to the rendezvous.

The rest of the vast air fleet of 113 Dakotas and 16 gliders had suffered a similar fate. The tight formations were broken up even before they had sighted the Sicilian coast. The planes took off in all directions and many missed their targets. Some soldiers were dropped in Southern Italy, others in the mountainous hinterland of Sicily and still more fell into the sea and were drowned. Less than twenty percent of the 1st Parachute Brigade were dropped according to plan and nearly thirty percent, through no fault of their own, returned to base without dropping. Twelve officers and 283 other ranks, out of a total of 1,856 all ranks who left North Africa, were available for the battle for which they were intended.

Those who actually arrived on the drop zone found the confusion on the ground equally monumental. Unknown to the British, the Germans had also sent in paratroops to reinforce their ground forces. So in the blazing cornfields, the vineyards and the olive groves, little groups of fighting men armed to the teeth cautiously moved around in the dark trying to find their friends. Often they found only their enemies. One paratrooper assembling his machine gun from its container was approached by a grey-smocked figure who asked him in German: 'Have you seen my Schmeisser?'

He said 'Nein' and then shot him.

Pearson's wireless operator, Bill Clarke, landed safely in a burning hayfield. As he ran towards an arms container he heard a rich tirade of curses behind him delivered in the unmistakable Glasgow accent of Alastair Pearson. Pearson, who had never mastered the art of parachuting, was having difficulty getting out of his harness. As Clarke helped to disentangle him, a burst of tracer scorched past them, setting more haystacks on fire. Pearson limped painfully into cover.

'Have you been hit, Sir?' asked Clarke anxiously.

'No, dammit,' said Pearson. 'Hold on a minute while I take this wretched thing off.'

He stopped at the edge of the field, ripped off a gaiter and painstakingly began to unwind a bandage from his left knee.

'My knee's a bit wonky and I put this on to protect it when I am jumping,' he explained to the astonished Clarke as he whipped off the last strand. 'Now let's get the hell out of here.' He stood up, his trouser leg flapping around his ankle, a revolver stuck gangster-style in his waistband and, miraculously, his black pipe sticking from his mouth. Pearson was ready for battle.

Meanwhile Captain Rann and about fifty men of the 1st Battalion had attacked the bridge and captured it. There had been few difficulties as the bridge was defended by Italians who seemed only too eager to surrender. About fifty were later taken prisoner. By first light their position on the bridge had been consolidated with about one hundred and twenty men now under Pearson's command.

The Brigade Commander, Brigadier Lathbury, had also jumped and had made his way to the bridge from the south side. He heard English voices coming from the area of the bridge and assumed it had been taken. As he approached the bridge a grenade was flung at him by a stray Italian and Lathbury became the recipient of a large chunk of shrapnel embedded in his backside. He put Pearson in command of the bridge, who at once set about organizing its defence. German explosives, which had been wired along the bridge ready to blow it up, had been cut off and thrown in the river. Grenade necklaces were strung across the road and slit trenches dug.

The paratroopers lay in their slit trenches and in the irrigation ditches of the olive groves and vineyards. They watched as the Germans prepared their counter-attack on the plains of Catania below. Long columns of trucks, packed with over 2000 German paratroops, wound their way cautiously forward along the white road towards the bridge. Behind them came the heavy armour, tanks and field guns. On the Catania airfield rows and rows of Messerschmitts stood in line having their machine guns loaded.

At 0630 hours on 14 July German paratroopers, supported by machine guns and heavy mortars, counterattacked the 2nd Battalion from the west. About an hour later a Forward Observation Officer, Captain Vere Hodge, contacted a British 6-inch gun cruiser, HMS *Mauritius*, that was lying offshore in direct support. By 1000 hours the cruiser had sent several accurate salvoes into the advancing Germans and the results were devastating. There were few left who could walk, and those who could beat a hasty retreat. But, unfortunately, then came the Messerschmitts. With brutal regularity, they flew up and down the valley, strafing the hiding men and returning to base to reload for another run.

Another attack was launched by the Germans at about 1300 hours. This built up throughout the afternoon, as German and Italian reinforcements were moved in to assist. Pearson moved to the edge of a vineyard to see the first German trucks arrive. He heard the faint sound of a song. The Germans were singing their battle song, *Lili Marlene*.

As the morning wore on more and more British paratroopers arrived at the position, as did more and more Italian prisoners. These latter soldiers milled around in their smart fawn uniforms, carrying their suitcases and shouting, 'Good old Tommy!' They were only too delighted to have been taken prisoner.

Finally, Pearson had a grand total of one hundred and sixty-four men, two mortars, three anti-tank guns and one machine gun. Somewhere in the hills around the bridge there were the remnants of two other parachute battalions covering the flanks. The southern approaches were firm, but the northern ones were wide open to attack. A much reduced 1st Parachute Brigade, with very few heavy weapons, and remarkably poor communications, had achieved its objective but was not in a good position to resist a strong enemy counter-attack. The expected early relief by the advancing ground formations was essential.

The Germans had several battalions of Panzers in Catania and a Luftwaffe fighter squadron of Messerschmitts armed with cannon and machine guns. Pearson crystallized his battle plans.

'Fight the barbarians off as long as possible,' he told his men.

As Pearson watched through his binoculars, one of his veteran sergeants from North Africa, Jock Rainnie, scrambled along a roadside ditch and lobbed a couple of hand grenades into the first two trucks, which exploded a couple of seconds later into great balls of orange flame. Screaming Germans fell on to the road and plunged into the river. Then there was silence.

The Germans dropped their trucks and spread out into the fields. They closed in both sides of the approach road to the bridge. Soon virtually every haystack concealed a German. Their snipers began to pick off Pearson's men one by one. His paratroopers steeled themselves for the first attack, but suddenly there was a strange interruption to the drama. As both sides tensed themselves for the fight an elderly Sicilian came riding down the road on an ancient bicycle, watched by hundreds of pairs of eyes. He zig-zagged round the German bodies that littered the road. As he passed Pearson standing in the bushes, he shouted a cheerful 'Buon Giorno'. Pearson politely tipped his helmet as the old man pedalled on across the bridge and out of sight.

Then the shooting began in earnest. It went on all day, with brief intervals when the Germans retreated a few hundred yards to allow their artillery to hammer the paratroopers. Pearson walked among his men encouraging them, totally indifferent to the bomb bursts and bullets which crashed about him. Occasionally he would stop and raise his binoculars to his eyes to watch the Germans creep across the fields.

By mid-afternoon he had lost about twenty men killed and about fifty wounded. But still he rallied his men, moving them around the bridge to counter each fresh German onslaught. The canny knack he had acquired in North Africa of knowing where the enemy would strike next had not deserted him. He brilliantly used the few men he had to blunt the point of each German thrust. Wherever the enemy massed for a final, devastating attack, they found Pearsn's paratroopers waiting to throw them back.

However, with each hammering assault the paratroopers were driven further and further into the tightening circle around the bridge, inexorably squeezed in the massive vice of the German hordes. By teatime Pearson could only keep his hold on the bridge by sweeping fire through the girders from a few pillboxes on the south bank of the river. The German attacks were now coming simultaneously from the north, the east and the south. To the west, the men of the 2nd Battalion were guarding his only line of retreat.

Pearson's outstanding leadership was again exemplified by the cool way he directed the fire of his gunners on the ground. By moving all over the battlefield, he could see where fire was most needed and avoided delays by issuing the fire orders himself.

'There's a bunch of them behind that haystack,' he would say to his mortar sergeant. 'Give them one in the neck.' Again he risked life and limb by commanding the battle up front.

The battle was so fluid that it required his presence everywhere at once. He found that, if he waited for the companies to pass back the information, his response, based on that information, was often out of date. He fought his battle the way he thought it should be fought rather than according to the text book. Warfare often requires the commander to get forward and see for himself. Pearson relished the excitement of the front, but was not reckless enough deliberately to provide the Germans with a target. By being seen he was able to keep the morale of his men up and at the same time look out for those soldiers who were finding the battle a strain.

As he wandered along the lines, he came upon one man, his rifle thrown aside, clutching his head.

'What's wrong?' asked Pearson, kneeling beside him.

'I've got a sore head,' said the man. 'The noise is driving me mad. I canna go on.'

Pearson straightened up and as he did so his boot flashed out.

'And now you've got a sore backside as well. Get on with your job.' The man, grinning, picked up his rifle again as a great roar of laughter came from his mates. A hundred yards away, the Germans listened to the mad *Britischers* enjoying a joke in the midst of battle, facing almost certain annihilation, and they shook their heads in amazement.

Throughout the day, the Germans returned over and over again as the sun scorched its afternoon path over the smoke-filled valley. They brought up a battery of anti-tank guns to take pot-shots at the pillboxes. Lieutenant Bob Gammon, a young officer from Glasgow, watched, hypnotized, as the guns ranged in on his pillbox. Suddenly he realized that the next shell would be right on target. He flung himself through the door as the shells ripped into it, the thick concrete chunks flying all around him. Dazed, he picked himself up out of the débris and staggered back over the bridge in a hail of rifle fire. A medical orderly stepped out from the surgical post at the side of the bridge and dragged him in for treatment.

The German advance was now so rapid that one paratrooper who was knocked out by a flying rock woke up several minutes later to find a German machine-gun post set up in the position where he had left his comrades. Pearson and his men, forced from the remaining pillboxes by crushing artillery fire, sprawled in the muddy reeds by the riverside.

For nearly two hours they made a defiant stand. Then the Germans set fire to the reeds to try and smoke them out. At 1705 hours, under heavy enemy pressure, all troops of the 1st and 2nd Battalions were withdrawn to the southern bank of the river, but, although decreasing amunition supplies prevented heavy fire being maintained against the Germans, the latter were still prevented from reaching the bridge itself.

Realizing that they could make no further progress from the front, the enemy kept up a murderous fire while crossing the river further to the east. By 1845 Pearson's situation on the bridge was becoming untenable as his position was now totally exposed due to the burning reeds. There was still no sign of relief and communications with the 2nd Battalion were cut. At 1935 Pearson was ordered to withdraw under cover of darkness and join up with the 2nd Battalion if possible. Slowly, carefully, they extracted themselves one by one from the stranglehold of the German forward positions. They left their dead behind, but carried as many of their wounded as they could. Painfully they made their way to the

2nd Battalion positions on a rocky ridge overlooking the bridge.

From the slopes they could see the triumphant Germans frantically trying to salvage the explosive charges from the river to blow up the bridge, but after one attempt they withdrew for the night. Pearson waited all night to see what would happen and nothing did. 'Not a bloody soul came near it!'

He sent his men back to rest but remained behind himself with his Provost Sergeant, 'Panzer' Manser, and his batman Jock Clements, hoping to see the 9th Battalion, the Durham Light Infantry finish the job. At 0800 hours the following morning, 15 July, the DLI attack went in, supported by tanks and fields guns. But it was, unfortunately, an unsuccessful and costly attack which should never have happened.

Later that day Pearson and Frost were at an informal orders group when they heard that the Durham Light Infantry intended repeating the attack at 1600 that afternoon. Pearson was there to act as a technical advisor to tell them about the ground. By this stage he was hungry and filthy and looked more like a tinker than a commanding officer. Without waiting to be asked his opinion, Pearson said in a loud voice but as if to himself, 'Well if you want to lose another bloody battalion that's the right way to do it.'

The Brigadier took this criticism in good part and turned to Pearson and said, 'All right Alastair, how would you do it?'

Pearson, without batting an eyelid, said, 'I think I could take that Battalion across the river tonight.' The Brigadier accepted his offer and told the Durham Light Infantry commander to work under Pearson.

Pearson remembered that, when he had withdrawn from the bridge the previous day, he had crossed at a fordable point about a mile upstream. He also knew that the Germans could not possibly cover all the river bank and that they were most likely to concentrate their forces near the bridge. The ground around the bridge was covered with scrub bushes

which had allowed the German snipers to get in close, so it
would give the new attacking forces the same cover.

Having made another reconnaissance in daylight, Pearson
then spoke to the Commanding Officer and the Company
Commanders of the Durham Light Infantry. He said, 'I will
take you across the river and put you on the bridge, but after
that you are on your own. I will cross that bridge and I'll be
up that road as hard as I can bloody well go!'

It was a classic Pearson manoeuvre – a night attack,
catching the enemy in the rear, a move he had carried out to
perfection in North Africa. The only thing he insisted upon
having was three miles of white tape. Soldiers moving in
columns at night have a habit of getting lost and to prevent
this Pearson was going to lay out a fool's guide.

They started off at midnight in line astern, headed by
Pearson's batman, Jock Clements, who knew the way. He
was followed by 'Panzer' Manser carrying the leading roll of
white tape. The Commanding Officer and three of the
Company Commanders went next with Pearson. 'They were
very distressed,' he later recalled, 'as they had never been so
near the front in their lives!'

They approached the river with very little noise, but
suddenly the night air was pierced by a single rifle shot. One
of the soldiers behind Pearson had just been shot through the
head by another soldier who had had an accidental discharge.
Everybody went to ground and waited for the Germans to
open up. But nothing happened. Pearson put this down to
the fact that in war there are solitary shots going off all the
time, and that the Germans must have assumed that it was
an accidental discharge, a problem that affects all armies.

After about five minutes they set off again and got down to
the river. Pearson turned to Jock Clements and said, 'Away
across that river.'

Clements turned round to his Commanding Officer and
asked incredulously, 'Me Sir?'

'Aye, you,' said Pearson. 'You know the way, don't you?'

So into the river waded Clements and stealthily made his

way to the far bank. There he sat down and waved his shaded torch back at Pearson that all was clear.

Pearson whispered as loud as he dared, 'Don't just wiggle that torch about. Away on and have a look around.'

Reluctantly Clements crept off into the scrub to look for any signs of the enemy. After about five minutes he came back and signalled the All Clear.

They all crossed the river and made their way down to the bridge. When they got there, there was nobody to be seen. Pearson then turned to the Commanding Officer, his job done, and said, 'Now, for heaven's sake get your men out to the edge of the scrub because they'll [the Germans] be here in the morning. You can guarantee that. Remember what happened to the other battalion.'

He then wished them good luck and set off back to his own Battalion. On the way back he met an aged priest who was investigating what all the noise had been about the previous day!

Pearson met up with the rest of the Battalion and they wearily climbed aboard the 3-ton trucks and headed off to Syracuse. On the way they were stopped by General Montgomery who was driving towards the bridge. Dishevelled and dirty, Pearson got out of his vehicle and greeted Montgomery.

'Ah, Pearson,' said Montgomery. 'I'm delighted to see you. You've made a big difference to my campaign.'

He then strode off to talk to Pearson's soldiers who were all sleeping in the back of their trucks. Behind Montgomery went one of his staff officers handing out packets of cigarettes, items which were desired most after a hard battle. After visiting all the trucks he had a chat with Pearson, discussing the campaign in Sicily.

After this brief interlude they headed on to Syracuse. Here Pearson addressed his men, or those who were left, 'We were represented when the Primosole Bridge fell. I don't think we have to admit defeat yet.'

Proudly he gripped his pipe between his teeth. But it began to tremble. The shaking carried on right through his body. He was about to have the first of many attacks of malaria.

He was sent back to hospital in Syracuse. While he was there some of the casualties came back from Catania. One of these was the Adjutant of the Durham Light Infantry Battalion which Pearson had led across the river to attack the Primosole Bridge. He was badly wounded, although able to talk. Pearson went over to his bedside to speak to him and see how he was. The Adjutant said, 'I was there when you told my Commanding Officer not to stay where he was, but to push out to the edge of the scrub. But as soon as you disappeared he changed everything. And by Christ we suffered.'

But the Durhams held the bridge, though they took very heavy casualties. Ironically, however, Montgomery had changed his plans and decided to advance up the centre of the island.

After spending about two weeks in hospital, Pearson was sent to a convalescent depot in North Africa, the 71st British General Hospital at Sousse. At the same time as he was recovering from malaria, he contracted problems with his knees which meant further hospitalization. Eventually, after a rest, he recovered and was posted to a new job as a General Staff Officer Grade 1 (Air) with 6th Airborne Division.

After some weeks wandering around Italy and North Africa, he eventually 'hitched' his way back to England, landing at Hurn airport on a cold day towards the end of November, 1943. The first person he bumped into was his old friend General Richard Gale, who was then commanding 6th Airborne Division. Gale took Pearson out for lunch and after they had eaten, mostly in silence, he turned to Pearson and said, 'Alastair, what are you going to be doing next?'

'I'm going as the G1 (Air),' replied Pearson.

'Do you want a battalion?' asked Gale.

'Yes,' said Pearson, who was itching to get back to command soldiers.

'Well I've just sacked a battalion commander,' said Gale, 'and I'm looking for his replacement. The battalion is not in good shape, but you can have it.'

Pearson accepted this new challenge with relish, while

Gale went and made a few telephone calls changing his posting order. As Pearson was saying farewell, about to go on leave, he turned to Gale and asked, 'Oh, by the way, who is the Brigade Commander?'

'Your old friend James Hill!' said Gale.

Pearson went off smiling to himself at the irony of the situation.

VIII

New Beginnings

Brigadier Hill had asked General Gale if he could have Pearson as the new Commanding Officer for the 8th Parachute Battalion. The Battalion was in poor shape and Hill needed a forceful and experienced officer who could train it ready for war. Pearson, in turn, found Hill a great commander to work for, 'as he always left me alone!' It was for precisely this reason that Hill had asked Pearson to take over, because he knew that he would carry out any mission that he was given and had far more experience than his other two battalion commanders.

The 8th (Midland Counties) Battalion was a new Parachute Battalion, consisting of young men who had never heard a shot fired in anger. They were very different from the hardened professionals Pearson had commanded in North Africa and Sicily.

The Battalion had also been badly shaken by a couple of training accidents that had occurred just before he joined them. On an exercise in Scotland, a stick of parachutists had jumped prematurely out of their aircraft while it was still flying over the Firth of Tay. The drop zone was to have been at Barry Buddon, but the soldiers on board had mistaken the lights reflecting off the water for the signal to jump. Out they went and ten of them were drowned. The only survivor was the Regimental Sergeant Major, who managed to swim to a sand bar and was picked up the next morning at daybreak. Later another aircraft crashed during a night exercise into the side of a hill near Hungerford and eight men were killed.

It was amid this atmosphere of bad luck and general misfortune that Pearson took command. The Battalion was based at Tilshead on the edge of Salisbury Plain. The camp itself was a collection of wooden huts, erected as temporary

accommodation during the First World War, but had somehow retained its status and survived into the Second.

The day of Pearson's arrival came and the whole Battalion
was on parade, waiting for him to appear. He turned up in
an old-fashioned staff car and got out. He was greeted by the
Battalion Second-In Command, Major John Marshall. Marshall would have been the Battalion Commander if Pearson
had not suddenly become available.

Pearson inspected the front rank and then returned to his
car. He stood on the folding steps, a feature of such vehicles,
and addressed the assembled troops.

'I have never seen such a shower in my whole life,' he said.

With that he got into his car and drove away. The effect
was devastating. Before he left, Pearson told Marshall that
he would return the following day and he expected everyone
to be in brand new uniforms, including the officers. The
Quartermaster belonged to that breed who believe that
'stores are for storing and issues is for issuing!' Nevertheless,
new uniforms were produced for everyone and the whole
Battalion spent the intervening twenty-four hours polishing
and scrubbing everything that did not move.

The next day Pearson returned and inspected the Battalion. Once he had seen all the troops, he returned to the front
and said to them: 'I am pleased to command you.'

He then proceeded to interview all the officers and non-
commissioned officers. Three company commanders were
returned to their original units, (RTUd). Many of the
sergeants were also RTUd. Pearson went on to promote
people on the spot to sergeant from lance corporal, and to
bring in young officers from outside to take over as company
commanders.

One young officer who managed to keep his command was
a Second Lieutenant from Edinburgh called Colin Brown.
He remembers being questioned by Pearson about the people
within his platoon. Luckily he knew his men, but quite a
number of other officers, who did not know their men, were
relieved of command. It was a ruthless but effective way of

bringing home the point that a commander must know his men.

Within six months the 8th Battalion was one of the best in the Division. In between there was a great deal of hard work and training done. Marshall briefed Pearson on everyone within the Battalion and proved to be an extremely loyal and helpful Second-in-Command. Pearson also went to see General Gale to request that the Battalion be spared visits from VIPs and senior officers for at least three months.

'Does this include your Brigade Commander?' asked Gale.

'Especially him!' said Pearson. As it turned out, James Hill took this news very well. He had no worries about Pearson and realized that these three months were crucial to get the Battalion working as a team.

They trained by working an eleven-day fortnight, with a forty-eight hour leave pass at the end. This system worked well and the men behaved themselves when outside barracks. Their only fault was a penchant for 'borrowing' vehicles to get themselves back to camp. These vehicles would always be left outside the Commanding Officer's office, undamaged. The local police would ring up Pearson the following day and arrange a collection time, knowing where the stolen cars were!

There were endless parachute exercises, during which the men could practice and perfect their various skills. Slowly, over the months, Pearson restored the confidence of the young men who faced the job of spearheading the liberation of Europe. He took them to a wood in Oxfordshire and here taught them the art of guerrilla warfare using live ammunition for the first time. They learned how to destroy tanks, blow up bridges, mine roads and how to kill silently, all skills that they would later put to good use in Normandy. They were gradually making the transition from boys into men.

It was while they were at Tilshead that the Battalion was honoured by a visit from the King George VI and Queen Elizabeth, the present Queen Mother. They were accompanied by the two Royal Princesses. It was a warm sunny day in May, 1944. The King and Queen split up in order to speak to as many of the soldiers as possible. The Queen was speaking to a group of soldiers from Support Company and she turned to a heavily camouflaged sniper and asked, 'And what is your name?'

'MacDonald, Ma'am,' replied the sniper.

'Oh, and where are you from?'

'Glamis, Ma'am' said MacDonald.

'Ah,' said the Queen. 'You'll be my ghillie's young boy.'

'That's right Ma'am,' replied MacDonald, a huge grin spreading across his darkened face.

This discovery made the Queen's day and as a result the Royal party stayed an extra hour and a half. The accompanying generals were convinced that Pearson had stage-managed the whole incident, but even he did not know where Mac-Donald was from in Scotland.

During Pearson's stay at Tilshead he met his future wife. General Gale had invited a number of officers from the Division to a party, including Pearson. At this party was a young woman called Joan Niven who went and spoke to Alastair, who was looking rather bored by the proceedings. From that moment on love blossomed and Alastair Pearson had courting to add to his list of commitments!

Joan Niven had been married before, but was now a widow, as a result of the war. Her former husband had been a Wing-Commander in the RAF. After his death, she was left with the task of bringing up two young daughters. She lived, at the time, in the village of Marden, in Marden Grange. This was conveniently en route to the Battalion's training area, so Pearson was able to combine business and pleasure.

Eventually Alastair proposed to Joan and she accepted. Joan suggested that, as it was wartime, they should have a short engagement and get married in the near future.

'The 8th of June seems alright to me,' she said. 'What do you say?'

Alastair, who knew about the proposed date for D Day, could not say, 'No' without arousing suspicion. So he agreed, knowing that this would be one wedding when the groom was going to be a trifle late. Invitations were sent out to the

Divisional Commander, the Brigade Commander and many others. Everyone replied saying that they would come and the pretence was maintained. On 4 June Pearson was given permission to tell his bride-to-be that there would be an unavoidable delay. Joan was very understanding and accepted it as one of the exigencies of war.

'Make sure you come back in one piece,' she told him as they parted, not knowing if they would ever see each other again.

IX

Normandy

The plan for D Day was based around a large front of five divisions which were to land on the beaches between Vara-ville in the west and Ouistreham in the east, due north of Caen. The American airborne divisions, the 82nd and 101st, were to parachute and airland into an area south east and west of the town of Sainte Mère Église. The 82nd was specifically tasked to capture crossing points over the River Merderet and use the River Douve as a blocking line in case the Germans deployed their reserves. The 101st Division was tasked to move to the beaches and help with the landings of the seaborne troops of VII US Corps.

In the east, the British 6th Airborne Division, commanded by General Richard Gale, was to parachute in on the night of D-1/D Day. They were to land to the east of Caen and take crossing points over the River Orne at Benouville and Ranville. After this they were to link up with the Commandos and then dominate the ground to the east of Caen and prevent any possible German counter-penetration.

3 Parachute Brigade, commanded by Brigadier James Hill, consisted of the 8th and 9th Parachute Battalions and the 1st Canadian Parachute Battalion; one section of the 4th Anti-Tank Battery, Royal Artillery; 3rd Parachute Squadron Royal Engineers; one troop of the 591st Parachute Squadron of the Royal Engineers and the 224th Parachute Field Ambulance.

This force was to drop east of the River Orne and the tasks allotted to the Brigade were twofold. Firstly they had to silence the Merville Battery overlooking the approaches to the D Day beaches and destroy five bridges over the River Dives at Varaville, Robehomme, two at Bures and one at Troarn. Secondly they had to deny the enemy the advantages

of the high ridge from Le Plein in the north to Troarn in the
south, thereby preventing German observation of the bridgehead and road access from the east. Once established, they
were then to carry out long-range patrols to the south to
disrupt enemy movements.

Pearson's Battalion had to destroy the two bridges at Bures
and the one east of Troarn. Having done that, they were then
to assist in forming the bridgehead by occupying an area
south of Le Mesnil.

Everything was prepared for the greatest invasion in
history. Late on the night of 5 June a great air fleet took off
from airstrips in the south of England. Soon after midnight
the planes droned over the French coast and D Day had
begun.

The paratroopers had been rehearsing their role for the
past six months. Pearson would now see whether his training
of a 'green' battalion had been good enough for the forthcoming tasks. He himself had been sent an extra large parachute
by General Gale, designed to lower him more slowly. His
knees were still very weak and any hard jolts would probably
put him out of the war and confine him to a desk job. His
last parachute descent had been into Sicily, nearly a year
before.

The men had known for forty-eight hours that they were
about to be thrown into battle and not one of his men went
missing when the time came to board the aircraft. Just before
they got on the aircraft, Pearson assembled the Battalion and
spoke to them. He began by relaying a message that had
been given to him by Brigadier Hill:

'Gentlemen, in spite of your excellent training and orders,
do not be daunted if chaos reigns. It undoubtedly will.'

Pearson then continued with a few key points. Firstly he
stressed the need for everyone to make for their objective,
come what may. He was adamant that soldiers should not
get side-tracked by fire fights with the enemy.

Then on a more humorous note he concluded:

'Men, do you know what your first action will be when you
land? You'll all have a pee!'

And sure enough, when they landed, the nervous paratroopers relieved themselves and then carried on with their
tasks!

When they landed there was undoubtedly chaos. After all,
it was the first time in history that an air invasion had been
attempted on such a scale. Nearly 10,000 men in two hundred
and sixty-six planes and three hundred and forty-four gliders
were to be landed in the heart of German-occupied territory
within twenty-four hours, complete with artillery, small arms,
ammunition, transport, medical equipment, food and 'all the
paraphernalia needed for modern warfare'.

Inevitably there were problems. Gliders got lost and planes
crashed; men landed miles from their objectives. Those who
did reach the drop zones faced terrifying hazards. Lifeless
bodies swung from the trees on their parachute lines, grim
evidence of the accuracy of German small-arms fire. Many
paratroopers dropped in swamps and rivers and were
drowned. Others were taken prisoner the moment they
touched the ground. The Germans lined up five Canadians
and shot them as spies, though one survived to tell the tale.

Major W. A. C. Collingwood, the Brigade Major, was
blown through a shell hole in his aircraft and dangled at the
end of his parachute rigging lines for half an hour before he
was dragged in again. He was taken back to England, but
later arrived in Normandy in a glider! The paratroopers were
hitting back with everything they had even as they fell. One
was wounded as he approached the ground, but he managed
to pull the pin out of a grenade and killed three Germans as
they were firing at him.

Corporal Albert Price, from Birmingham, landed on the
top of a low building and broke his ankle. As he climbed
painfully from the roof, he heard German voices. Peering in
a window, he saw a conference of German staff officers.
Quietly he pulled the pin from a grenade and lobbed it into
the group. They died instantly.

A certain Sergeant Jones snatched a Schmeisser from one
of his German captors and managed to kill eight of them
before escaping. Another had a more pleasurable experience:

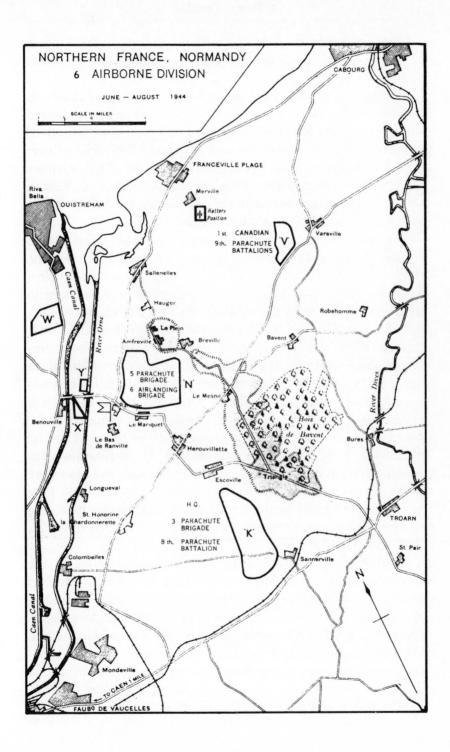

NORTHERN FRANCE, NORMANDY
6 AIRBORNE DIVISION

JUNE — AUGUST 1944

SCALE IN MILES

CABOURG

FRANCEVILLE PLAGE

Riva
Bella

OUISTREHAM

Merville

Battery
Position

1st. CANADIAN
9th. PARACHUTE
BATTALIONS

'V'

Varaville

Sallenelles

Caen Canal

Hauger

Robehomme

'W'

River Orne

Le Plein

Breville

Bavent

Amfreville

Y

5 PARACHUTE
BRIGADE

6 AIRLANDING
BRIGADE

'N'

Le Mesnil

Benouville

N

Ranville

'X'

Le Mariquet

Le Bas
de Ranville

Bois
de Bavent

River Dives

Bures

Herouvillette

Escoville

Triangle

Longueval

St. Honorine
la Chardonnerette

H.Q.

3 PARACHUTE
BRIGADE

8th. PARACHUTE
BATTALION

'K'

TROARN

St. Pair

Colombelles

Sannerville

N

Caen Canal

Mondeville

TO CAEN 1 MILE

FAUBᴳ DE VAUCELLES

he was knocked out when he fell. When he awoke, he was gazing into the eyes of a beautiful French girl who was bending over him. She put him on the back of her tandem bicycle and took him to rejoin his unit. All over the battlefield similar scenes were happening as the paratroopers fought their way to their rendezvous and gathered to attack their various targets.

A fierce battle raged at the bridge over the Caen canal – later to be rechristened 'Pegasus Bridge'. Also, an heroic struggle was being fought to silence the huge coastal battery at Merville, which menaced the Allied beaches.

Pearson's Battalion dropped over a wide area of farmland, west of the town of Troarn, a few miles from Caen and some twelve miles inland. 'P' (Parachute) hour* for Pearson and his men was 0050 hours on 6 June. Pathfinders and a Rendezvous Reconnaissance Party had been dropped half an hour earlier. Despite these aids to navigation, Pearson had a further plan. He knew that night parachute operations invariably developed into chaos as soon as the red light went on, as often the aircraft were in the wrong area. He instructed his RV party to fire Verey flares in the sky as soon as they heard the aircraft approaching. He had also instructed the pilots to drop his men in the area of the flares. 'This way,' he explained, 'we can all be lost together!' This could only work provided the RV party was not surrounded by the enemy— which it was not.

Pearson and his Battalion met up with their respective aircrews a couple of days before the operation. Virtually all the crews were under twenty-one years old except Pearson's own crew. They were all at least fifty years old if they were a day! However, once Pearson had talked to his pilots and navigator, he was very glad that he had them in control of his aircraft. They were all Canadians and had been bush pilots in the Canadian outback before the war. His pilot was also the Squadron Leader and was extremely suspicious of the 'loose talk' that was pervading the other crews.

---

* The time an aircraft is one over the Dropping Zone.

The younger pilots thought it was simple to find the drop zones, but as the senior Canadian pilot explained, dropping paratroopers was not as easy as it appeared.

'It's very hard, but you try telling these guys,' he said. 'Unless I can make an accurate landfall on the coast of France, there's no way I can drop you on your DZ, and you have the greatest problem as you are getting dropped further inland than anyone else.'

He then explained that with the vast numbers of aircraft that would be in the sky that night, he would be unable to circle and try for a second drop. The airforce plan was bound to be a difficult one, as they had so many different types of aircraft; Albemarles, Dakotas, Stirlings, Halifaxes. . . . They all had different cruising speeds and the faster ones were going to have to wait for the slower ones to catch up.

They took off at about 2230 hours and headed up to Yorkshire where the great armada formed up. After they had been flying for half an hour, the navigator came back to speak to Pearson:

'We are all right now, Sir,' he said.

'How's that?' asked Pearson, somewhat puzzled.

'We've lost the other two from our formation!' said the navigator. Pearson looked askance.

'Don't worry, Sir,' continued the navigator. 'I know where we are, even if no one else does.'

As it was, all the aircraft had to fly over Odiham, which was lit up for the night to aid navigation.

Going across the Channel they ran into a hailstorm, but it was short-lived. The hailstones sounded like bullets hitting the side of the Dakota. The weather had cleared by the time they approached the coast of France. The Intelligence Officer leaned out of the door, trying to see where they were. He yelled back inside the aircraft to Pearson, 'We're right on it,' referring to the route to the drop zone.

They dropped about three miles from Troarn. It was a cornfield, with the crop standing about two foot high. Apart from the corn there were no other obstacles as there were on many of the other drop zones.

In his briefing Pearson had stressed the need for the maintenance of the mission. He said, 'Even if you meet Rommel in person, you must press on and get to the bridge with your weapon.' This directive paid tremendous dividends in the early stages of the battle.

Pearson was hit in the hand almost as soon as he hit the ground by one of his own men who had an accidental discharge with his Sten gun. Although the wound was intensely painful, it was nearly twenty-four hours before he could be persuaded to have the bullet extracted.

He reached the rendezvous and was met by the RV party, who were all there. The officer in charge of the RV party informed Pearson that only about fifty men had reported in. This was far fewer than he had hoped for. As there were fewer soldiers than planned, Pearson sent a patrol into Troarn to see what the situation was like in the town. They returned about an hour later and reported that there was a manned road block just outside the town, but, as far as they could see, there was a fair number of enemy within the town. The numbers were too great for Pearson's meagre fighting force. All units were represented, but some only by one man. The Sappers, for example, had one man instead of two Troops. The whole force numbered about one hundred and fifty.

With the maintenance of the mission in mind, Pearson summoned the sole Sapper, a lance-corporal, and told him that he was now the engineer adviser. The Sapper. then proceeded to present his plan. Each soldier carried one pound of plastic explosive, so there were at least one hundred and fifty pounds of explosive within the group— sufficient to blow a hole in a bridge.

Pearson then formed a composite platoon and briefed the platoon commander. He told him that the bridge at Troarn was not heavily defended, a couple of sentries at either end. A second composite platoon was also formed to go and deal with the bridge at Bures. After dividing the explosive, they set off for their respective targets. Both bridges had to be blown by 0900 hours at the latest. Pearson left a lance-corporal and four men on the road with three PIAT (Projector Infantry Anti-Tank) guns and told them to stop any enemy who came along the road.

Alastair then set off for a cross-tracks in a wood, where he had planned to set up his Headquarters. Just after he arrived at the cross-tracks, he heard the sounds of a major fire fight back on the road where he had left the half section. He sent a soldier to investigate. When the soldier returned, he found out that the Germans had attempted to move a sizeable force along the road. The section had destroyed three half-tracks and killed about a dozen soldiers. The rest of the group had fled.

Some days later Pearson discovered from some German prisoners that the fleeing enemy had reported a considerable force on the road, including many anti-armour weapons. It is possible that this report caused the Germans to think twice about their plan to take the beaches.

Meanwhile, just before 0900 hours, an enormous explosion shattered the quiet morning air. It was followed a few seconds later by a second. The first explosion had come from the direction of Bures and the second from Troarn. The bridge at Bures had been blown by the company who were originally tasked to do the job. They had dropped on the wrong drop zone. Realizing their predicament, they set off immediately for the objective, rather than waste time trying to find the rendezvous. At the bridge they had met little resistance and had carried out their part of the plan perfectly.

The second explosion from Troarn was a result of the lost engineers reaching to the bridge by a very circuitous route. The Sappers, commanded by Major J. C. A. Roseveare, were also dropped on the wrong drop zone. However, as they landed with all their equipment, things were not as bad as they at first appeared. They had recovered a glider-borne jeep and filled it with Beehive explosive charges, and then eight of them climbed aboard and set off in the direction of Troarn. They were all armed to the teeth with Sten and Bren guns.

Not knowing where anybody else was, they drove as fast as they could along the road in the dark. They drove straight through Pearson's road block and sped on towards Troarn. Major Roseveare put his foot down and drove along the main street. The men on board blazed away with their machine guns at anything that moved. The Germans did not know what had hit them and a few desultory shots were all that they could offer in return.

They emerged on the other side of the town and plunged down a steep hill to the bridge, with a hail of machine-gun bullets whistling around their ears from the bridge guards. The sight of the jeep thundering down the road with guns ablaze was too much for the Germans and they disappeared at once.

Brakes screeching, the jeep pulled to a halt and the Sappers jumped off and placed their Beehive charges, got back into the jeep and sped off again. About two minutes later an enormous explosion ripped a twenty-foot gap in the bridge. They were out of sight before the enemy realized that they were not being attacked by a regiment. Shortly afterwards, Colin Brown and his composite platoon arrived at the bridge and increased the size of the gap.

By about 1000 hours on D Day the strength of Pearson's Battalion had risen to about four hundred. Throughout the remainder of the day men continued to arrive at the Headquarters, which proved how thorough the briefings had been back in England.

Pearson then set about convincing the Germans in Troarn that his numbers were greater than they really were. He sent out heavily armed fighting patrols to take the war to the enemy. Over the next ten days they harassed the Germans all over the countryside. They slept during the day, hidden by the thick foliage of the Bois de Bavent, and went out at night to keep the Germans awake.

Their impudence became so daring that many of the paratroopers were able to visit Troarn at night to be entertained by the jubilant French citizens in their homes, right under the noses of the Germans. They roamed the streets

shooting up German patrols, hurling grenades through bar-
rack windows and generally creating alarm and despondency
in the enemy ranks. All around the area, Pearson directed his
forces to blow craters in the roads and cripple German lines
of communication in every way possible.

During the afternoon of D+2, while the Battalion was
resting up, through the trees came a bedraggled-looking
figure. It was the Regimental Sergeant-Major of the 13th
Parachute Battalion. He went up to Pearson and saluted. He
explained that on the other side of the River Dives, in a farm,
was a group of wounded soldiers. A Dakota had crashed
during the original drop and there were fourteen survivors
who were sheltering in a barn. Having listened to his story,
Pearson took the RSM back down the road to Brigade
Headquarters to see James Hill, the Commander. Pearson
recounted the RSM's story and added: 'We had better go
and get them.'

'And just who is going to go and get them?' asked Hill.

'I'll go and get them, if it's all right with you,' said
Pearson. He went on, 'I'll go for two reasons. Firstly, I have
got no one else who could go, and secondly, I've got more
experience than anyone else.'

Hill then asked Pearson who he was going to take with
him.

'My mortar platoon. I'll take my donkeys as they are the
fittest and strongest and will be able to carry the heavy
loads,' he explained. Hill agreed to the plan and wished them
luck.

That night, under cover of darkness, they set off. They had
a jeep with them to act as an ambulance. They moved
through the woods towards Bures. Pearson knew from intelligence reports that there was a glider sitting in the river near
Bures, and he also knew that all gliders had an inflatable
dinghy on board. His plan was to use the dinghy and thus
save everyone from getting their feet wet. They parked their
jeep out of sight, got the dinghy out of the glider and
proceeded to inflate it. This took at little time, but after
twenty minutes they were ready to cross the river.

The first soldier jumped into the dinghy with his bayonet fixed to his rifle. As he stepped into the boat, he stuck the blade into the side and it began to sink. Everyone else stood on the bank staring in disbelief as the dinghy slowly sank. As soon as the soldier had scrambled from the water, Pearson kicked him as hard as he could in the backside and the man ended back in the river. The soldier emerged dripping.

'You can't do that, Sir,' he gasped to Pearson. 'Its against King's Regulation. I'll complain to the Brigadier.'

'You can complain to General-bloody-Montgomery himself,' raged Pearson. 'For your stupidity you can stay here until we come back, to guide us across the river again. And if a German patrol comes to find out what all this bloody row is about . . . well, good luck to you.'

A second dinghy was found in the glider and eventually the patrol continued across the river to the sleeping village on the other side. Pearson split his men and took a party forward to the farm where the injured airmen and paratroopers were being sheltered. At the farm they were met by a wizened old French woman who had been looking after the injured men. None of them was fit to walk. Some had broken legs, others broken ribs and one RAF warrant officer had a very serious head wound.

As his men treated the wounded, Pearson tackled the problem of moving the men back to safety. Finally, after some searching of the farm buildings, he pointed to an enormous farm cart which stood at the end of the barn. It had great wooden wheels and huge shafts.

'We'll take that,' he said. The old woman indicated that there were no animals left to pull the cart.

'We'll haul it ourselves,' said Pearson.

He offered the old woman several thousand Francs as a reward for her help. Proudly, she refused to take it. Later she found the money lying under a cloak in her farm house. Pearson pulled the harness straps over his shoulders and ordered his men to buckle him into the shafts.

The injured men were loaded on to the cart and the strangest ambulance of the war trundled through the farm

7. Bures Bridge, Normandy, 1944.

8. Troarn Bridge, Normandy, 1944.

9.
Joan and Alastair
on their wedding day.

10.
Alastair in 1945,
aged 30.

11. A cartoon of Alastair Pearson
when he was Commanding Officer
of a Reserve Battalion in 1946;
drawn by his Intelligence Sergeant,
Sergeant S. G. Anderson.

12. Alastair Pearson with his dog Meg in 1982.

gates and out on to the road. Then came a new problem as the cart creaked and grumbled back towards the silent village. There was always, of course, the danger of being surprised by a German patrol, but Pearson was even more worried about the other half of his own patrol, with whom he had lost contact, especially as it was commanded by a Corporal McGurk, a man known to shoot first and ask questions later!

It was not inconceivable that they might mistake the noisy approach of Alastair's ambulance for the advance of a German column and attack their comrades in the dark. The dilemma was solved with typical Pearson inspiration. As the cart skidded into the main street of the village, he shouted to his men: 'Let's have a song!'

The paratroopers were mystified. But orders were orders and Pearson was not a man to disobey.

The village was suddenly wakened by a raucous chorus of 'Roll out the barrel'. The astonished villagers left their beds to peep through their curtained windows at the crazy caravan careering down the street. They were tackling an uproarious third verse when Corporal McGurk from the lost section tackled them.

'It's just as well you let us know it was you, Colonel,' he said to Pearson. 'We thought you were a tank and were all set to knock hell out of you!'

They pressed on, this time in comparative silence, and some hours later the patrol carried the wounded men through the German lines to the safety of Pearson's Headquarters deep in the forest. All the men survived.

Every couple of days the Battalion would move position to prevent the Germans finding out where exactly in the wood they were. The paratroopers were fighting the kind of war for which they were specially trained and which they liked best. Pearson was christened 'Monarch of the Woods'. Like a defiant stag, he dared the Germans to invade his territory.

Each day the Germans blasted the forest with artillery, mortars and their new and frightening weapon, the *Nebelwerfer*. This was a deadly multi-barrelled rocket launcher whose rockets shrieked as they crashed through the trees.

Pearson refused to be intimidated. Each morning he ate breakfast, served by his batman, at a table in a shed which was a make-shift officers' mess. All around his head swarmed thousands of mosquitoes, but he seemed oblivious to them. Captain Denis Kelland remembers that Pearson ordered all the officers to eat in the 'Mess' when operations permitted.

'One day a number of us were seated round a trestle table . . . doing full justice to our rations and talking of a variety of things when, without warning, there were sounds of a not-very-distant burst of Spandau fire and a hail of bullets came through the wall, passed between our heads and went out through the other wall. Almost to a man, we dropped to the floor beneath the table. The noise of a knife and fork upon a plate, however, soon told us that one man was getting on with his meal undisturbed. No one needed telling who that one man was. From the floor beneath the other end of the table came a voice asking: "Are you not going to join us down here, Sir?" From a mouth full of food came back the answer: "Och, ye canna dodge a bloody bullet!"'

Later on in the morning he held an orders group for his company commanders out in the open. Afterwards, men charged with breaches of discipline were marched in front of Pearson, and their sergeant-majors rapped out the evidence of their misdeeds. All the time the ground shook as the German shells continued to explode around the position. The men soon learnt that it was better to behave themselves than run the gauntlet of Pearson's court.

On 12 June the Germans made a last desperate attempt to drive the 3rd Parachute Brigade off the ridge. The 9th Battalion fought a running battle with the Germans who were supported by both tanks and 88mm guns. At one stage their defensive position was briefly penetrated. The Black Watch, who were defending the Château St Come alongside the 9th Battalion position, were driven back and Brigadier Hill was forced to collect any reserves he could find from the Canadian Battalion next door and from Brigade Head-quarters. He led a counter-attack to restore the position left as a result of the Black Watch withdrawal.

At the same time Colonel Bradbrook's Canadians were being heavily attacked, both astride the Le Mesnil crossroads and on their right flank, where the company there was penetrated by German tanks which fired at their company headquarters in the brickworks at close range. In this battle for the Château St Come and Le Mesnil crossroads the enemy were driven off and suffered grievous losses.

Just before first light on 12 June Pearson alerted his troops.

'I think the Germans will attack this morning,' he told his officers. 'I feel it in my bones.'

One young officer had the temerity to be sceptical: 'How can you possibly tell, Sir?'

'Laddie,' said Pearson. 'I know about these things. Now put your tin hat on and warn your men.'

The German attack came in at first light. They pounded the paratroopers' trenches and then sent a horde of troops across the fields into the forest. Pearson was everywhere at once. Dashing through the exploding front, he roamed the trenches, urging his men to repel the attack. But soon the overwhelming numbers of Germans began to tell. They flooded through the gaps in the company lines and threatened to overrun the Battalion. Behind the waves of German infantry came the large 88mm guns, firing straight into the British troops. They continued to advance.

Pearson gathered a platoon of men.

'Follow me,' he commanded.

They charged up to one of the guns, annihilating the crew and took it over. Then they turned it round on the Germans. They sent shells tearing through the ranks of the German infantry and on to the remaining guns. In a few minutes the tide of battle had been completely turned. Bloodied and terrified, the Germans turned and ran.

For a week the paratroopers held out, defeating every German effort to destroy them. Slowly but surely, the Allies tightened their grip on the beachhead and fought through to the paratroopers. The 8th Battalion was finally joined by units of the 51st Highland Division. The German counter-attacks became weaker and fewer; the front line became static with the two armies facing each other across a battered strip of No-Man's-Land.

For two months the Germans held back the straining Allied armies and the war became an adventurous summer game of quick raids behind the enemy lines by opportunist patrols. But for the men in the trenches life became a tedious round of watching and waiting, sleeping and eating. Often the summer silence over the front made it difficult to tell if, in fact, the enemy was still there. And from Battalion Headquarters came the dreaded order to the platoons in the front line: 'Find out if the enemy trenches are still occupied.'

This meant that someone had to expose himself in No-Man's-Land to draw fire from the other side.

The order came one day to Lieutenant Colin Brown's platoon. Choosing a man for the job was an agonizing decision for a young commander. It was not easy to tell a man to risk his life in a cold and deliberate way. A podgy Corporal, who had been saved from arrest for bigamy because Pearson would not let the police enter the camp before D Day, relieved the young lieutenant of the responsibility by volunteering.

'I don't mind having a look, Sir' he said. 'It can't be any worse than facing two wives at the same time!'

He heaved himself out of his trench and ambled untidily over the battlefield. The rest of the Platoon held their breath and watched. The Corporal walked straight up to the German trenches. He stopped to peer in one and then pulled a couple of grenades from his belt and dropped them into the holes in the ground like a man scrambling eggs. He was on his way back to the trenches when the explosions came and the battlefield erupted violently. Through a wall of fire, the fat Corporal walked steadily on. He dropped into the trench beside Lieutenant Brown.

'They're still there,' he reported laconically. 'They were just having their afternoon nap!'

One day in early August Pearson and two sergeant-majors went up to Divisional Headquarters to see General Gale.

Pearson was trying to get both his men battlefield commissions. They walked in to see Gale, who had already been told the details by 3 Parachute Brigade. He turned to the two warrant officers and said, 'If you're good enough for Alastair Pearson, you're good enough for me.'

Within twenty-four hours their commissions were confirmed.

After the men had left, Gale turned to Pearson and said, 'Drink?' Both men then set about the bottle of scotch and discussed the war.

Pearson stayed for dinner with Gale and, after a few more 'drams', Pearson felt that he was up to doing the General's job! They were discussing the present stalemate within the area and various ways in which it could be overcome. Gale invited Pearson to set out in detail his plan for a possible breakout. This Pearson did and thought no more about the matter. Unbeknown to him the GSO1, called Bobby Bray, had been listening to the plan and took copious notes.

About three days later Pearson was summoned to Hill's headquarters and was told that the 8th Battalion would be leading the breakout of the 3rd Parachute Brigade. Hill then handed Pearson a copy of the plan. There in black and white was Pearson's plan to the letter. Hill added, 'I suppose that's what you and the Divisional Commander were discussing the other night?'

'Oh no, Sir,' said Pearson. 'We were just chatting.'

Hill had his doubts but kept them to himself.

The 8th Battalion had been pulled into reserve about half a mile behind their original position to rest and recuperate for a couple of days. They had to break out through the wood and then through some marshes. The marshes were dominated by some high ground to the south and Pearson was convinced that the Germans were bound to have considerable forces on the ridge so as to prevent such an allied action.

He went with his point platoon who led the Battalion cautiously across the marshes and approached the high ground with trepidation, expecting to be cut to pieces at any moment. But no fire came their way. It transpired that the

Germans had moved further back than any of the allies had anticipated. The only enemy fire they encountered was some desultory gunfire from a German 88mm.

By mid-morning on 17 August Pearson and his men had crossed the marshes and were able to secure the high ground. By that same evening 3 Parachute Brigade had reached the area of Goustranville after some heavy fighting. The following evening 3 and 5 Parachute Brigades, along with 4 Special Service Brigade, were concentrated on an island in the river near Troarn. At 2200 hours on 18 August 3 Parachute Brigade attacked the four main bridges over the Dives canal and had captured these by 0220 hours the following morning.

Early on 21 August, 3 Parachute Brigade started their advance north-east towards the town of Pont L'Evêque, well to the east of Caen. 'Here we took a hammering,' says Pearson. The fighting was fierce, but Pearson led his men in the advance, fighting for cross roads, houses, railway bridges. They battled their way with tanks, cleaned out blazing villages which the Germans had set alight.

At one tiny village called Annebault, too small to appear on a map, they were held up by 'another of those bloody 88 guns!' The gun was well sited and was able to move around with its half-track. The Germans also employed a *Nebelwerfer* which was very inaccurate, but one rocket did find its mark and exploded in Battalion Headquarters, killing a number of soldiers. The Battalion suffered more casualties after the breakout and the advance to the Seine than they did on the initial D Day landings.

The breakout continued, pressing the Germans back until they were on the Seine, which was where Pearson had his last battle during the Normandy phase of the war. For his part in the operation, he was awarded his fourth DSO. The citation simply reads: 'For outstanding courage and devotion to duty. . . . His conduct was an inspiration to the whole battalion.'

X

Marriage and Demobilisation

The 6th Airborne Division returned to England at the beginning of September, 1944. With them went the remaining men of the 8th Parachute Battalion. Alastair Pearson was still their Commanding Officer and had led them through all the fighting from D Day onwards. By now they were battle-hardened but weary men who had been in action for three months, virtually non-stop.

As they disembarked at Southampton, Pearson was greeted by his batman, who had gone ahead with the advance party.

'Good morning, Sir,' he said. 'You're getting married on Saturday!'

Pearson's face was a mixture of pleasure, because he quite liked the idea, and stubborn refusal because no one was going to tell him what to do.

'Oh no, I'm not,' he snapped back.

'I think you'll find you are, Sir. It's all arranged,' came the reply.

'I can't get married unless my mother is here,' retorted Pearson, still not in control of the situation.

'She's here, Sir,' replied his batman, grinning from ear to ear.

So he boarded the train to Marden and, a few days later, on 9 September, 1944, Joan Niven became Mrs Alastair Pearson. A large percentage of the Battalion had turned up to wish them both well and the festivities went on far into the night. All afternoon and most of the night, a piper, in full Highland dress, marched up and down the quiet main street of the village while the astonished villagers stared and gossiped.

'What's the celebration about?' asked a stranger.

'Oh,' replied a villager. 'It's only some mad Scotsman whose got himself a civilized English girl for a wife!'

While the rest of the Battalion returned to Bulford to prepare for their next assignment, Pearson had to resign himself to the fact that, for him, the war was over. After three years of superhuman effort and incredible bravery his health finally broke. He had recurring malaria which was exacerbated by the fighting in and around the marshes of Normandy. Brigadier James Hill remembers that, when they returned to England in September, Pearson was 'as yellow as a canary'. Even Pearson himself realized that his days of leading men into battle were over. He went to see Hill and said that, although he realized that other operations would be coming up, it would be selfish to himself as well as to the men under his command if he remained in his post.

He was posted as Commanding Officer of a reserve battalion stationed at Beverley in Yorkshire. There he passed on his immense fund of practical knowledge to the new recruits who were destined for service overseas.

He was offered the chance to stay on in the army as a regular officer, but he declined the offer. He realized that the end of the war was not too far away and that men like him, who made up their own rules as they went along, would find difficulty adjusting to life in a peacetime army. Instead he returned to his old career of baking. This was not a job he particularly enjoyed, but as they had paid him his salary throughout the war, he felt a certain obligation to return.

After about four years of baking, his asthma began to get worse, not helped by the flour dust in the bakery. He decided to visit a specialist he knew in Slough and get a medical opinion and advice on what future employment he should pursue. After the check-up, the doctor looked at him and said, 'Well, Alastair. You can go into industry and earn £5000 a year ... and I give you ten years before you are dead. Or, you can earn £500 a year in the country and you should see seventy.'

Pearson took this advice and decided to go into farming.

His wife had always had a yearning to farm and so they set
about looking for a farm. Eventually they found a lovely
place on the southern shores of Loch Lomond, in the country,
but close enough to her children's school in Glasgow. Here,
at a village called Gartocharn, they established a new home
in a farm called Tullochan, where they still live to this day.

XI

Post-war Service

It was inconceivable to think that Alastair Pearson would sever his military connections after he left the army. In 1947 he was given the opportunity of raising a Territorial Army battalion in Glasgow, which offer he gladly accepted, for there was still a great need for a large peacetime reserve army.

He formed the 15th (Scottish Volunteer) Battalion, the Parachute Regiment, based in his old drill hall in Yorkhill Street. This upset a few of the more established Glasgow Regiments, but Pearson was unrepentant. His confidence was more than justified and the Battalion is still very well recruited. Many Scottish ex-paratroopers rallied to join the new Battalion and there was soon a considerable wealth of talent and experience. He commanded the Battalion as a TA soldier for six years and for his outstanding work was awarded the Order of the British Empire.

After relinquishing command on 10 November, 1953, he moved to the Brigade Headquarters of 44 Independent Parachute Brigade, Territorial Army, as Training Colonel and Deputy Commander. He was a great adviser on matters concerning the TA, 'and in training generally was of tremendous assistance to his regular Brigade Commanders. During the summer camps he was, as ever, indefatigable, and as a chief umpire he was without peer. All who took part in the Brigade exercises will remember the rather shaggy figure, always in shirt-sleeve order, whatever the weather might be, driving himself in a Champ with great aplomb and skill from one scene of action to another.' He remained with 44 PARA Brigade until 1963 when he was made Honorary Colonel of 15 PARA (SV), a post which he held until 1977 and resumed again in 1983.

In 1967 he was promoted to Brigadier and became Com-
mandant of the Army Cadet Force in Scotland. This job
might, to the layman, seem lower key, but he injected as
much enthusiasm into it as into every other post he had held.

Outside the military sphere he has held appointments that
have kept him busy and mean that, even today, he is still
working as hard as ever. In 1951 he was made a Deputy
Lord-Lieutenant for Glasgow. He remained with Glasgow
until 1975 when he moved to Dunbartonshire, still as Deputy
Lieutenant. In 1979 he became Her Majesty's Lord-
Lieutenant of Dunbartonshire and, at the same time, Keeper
of Dumbarton Castle. His work as Lord-Lieutenant is extensive and he rarely turns down requests to appear at the
numerous functions and activities that occur in the county.
Even today, in his mid-seventies, he is still performing over
three hundred duties every year.

In addition to all his other work, he has maintained close
links with the Erskine Hospital, Glasgow. He joined the
Executive Committee of the Princess Louise Scottish Hospital
for Disabled ex-Servicemen in 1947. The Erskine Hosptial,
as it is known, is a voluntary body maintained by public
subscriptions. He has continued to take an interest in the
welfare of the patients and residents as well as attend to his
committee duties. Since 1980 he has been Vice-Chairman of
the Executive Committee and to this post 'he has brought
strong leadership drawn from his intimate knowledge of the
hospital'.

Alastair Pearson, postwar, has led a fascinating and full
life. But in December, 1983, he became very ill and was on
the critical list. Many of his friends thought that this was to
be his last battle. However, it will take more than one serious
illness to make Alastair Pearson retire from the fray. He
rallied and when he eventually returned home from hospital
he kindly agreed to let me write his extraordinary life story.

There have been few men this century who displayed such
leadership as he did. On countless occasions he was called
upon and was never found wanting. His immense physical
and moral courage have been an inspiration to soldiers both

in and out of conflict and he has been an example to many. It is perhaps ironic that such a man has shunned the publicity machine that exists today and prefers to live in modest semi-retirement. To many people, both past and present, he is perhaps the personification of a true soldier, a *warrior par excellence*.

Leadership

Leadership is studied in great detail at Sandhurst and during my two years there as an instructor, as well as my fifteen years' service with The Parachute Regiment, I have learned to recognize good and bad leaders. As I wrote this biography I compared the achievements of Alastair Pearson with the requisite qualities of leadership that the British Army now demands of its young officers. He fulfils all the qualities to a degree that might seem virtually impossible today. Yet I believe that he was a classic example of the right man in the right place at the right time.

Pearson had tremendous personal courage and displayed this on countless occasions throughout the war. The citations for each of his four DSOs mention his 'outstanding courage'. It was this courage that inspired the men under his command to fight that little bit longer and harder and overcome all difficulties. modern commanders may be forgiven for criticizing his seemingly reckless behaviour when under enemy fire. But Pearson realized that soldiers look to their officers most when enemy action is at its height and the dangers are greatest. Many of his officers were wounded or killed trying to emulate him, but he had an enormous amount of luck and survived when many others did not.

He had been trained in the Territorial Army in the various phases of war and he had the knowledge to train his soldiers properly, correct weakness and apply his military acumen to the modern battlefield. He knew his soldiers well and was able to get the last ounce of courage and energy from them, when events seemed to be about to overwhelm them. He was a robust leader and was prepared to motivate the idle and stupid with physical persuasion when required. Again, modern peacetime commanders may have difficulty in sympathizing with this sort of behaviour, yet at the time the well-aimed boot produced instant results.

Pearson was an honest soldier and demanded high standards of integrity from those who held authority under him. His sacking of a sergeant-major exemplifies his intense dislike of those who abuse their own position for personal gain. Again he admired those with the honesty to admit that they were not up to the task and resign.

Finally, his determination to succeed overcame many obstacles and it resulted in a number of battles won when they were so nearly lost. He has never accepted second-best and strives to achieve the highest standard in all that he sets out to accomplish. Throughout the war he and his fellow paratroopers were tested to the limit, yet his firm and resolute leadership often turned the tide of battle when lesser men would have given up hope.

Pearson was a leader who had little time for the established form of doing things. Red tape and staff work had its place, he acknowledged, but not near him. He may have looked extremely scruffy, swore when he was angry and used his boot when he saw fit, but his soldiers loved him all the more for it. He led by example, setting the highest standards of devotion and leadership. As Peter Cleasby-Thompson once said: 'We'd have followed him to the ends of the earth, regardless of the danger or outcome.'

I have included a lecture on Leadership that Alastair Pearson has given in various forms over the years. Some of his examples have been included in the main text of the book, but I have endeavoured to keep the majority of anecdotes in his lecture.

The text of a lecture
often given by Alastair Pearson

Leadership can be defined in its very broadest sense with a quote by Field-Marshal Lord Wavell given before the last war to universities. He said;

'We think and speak of the greatest captains and military operators like Hannibal, Napoleon and Marlborough. Let us add one more to that number. That is the good company, platoon or section commander who leads forward his men or holds his post and often falls unknown. It is they who in the end do most to win wars. The British are a free people and this tradition of freedom gives our junior leaders in war the priceless gift of initiative.'

Now, what is leadership? Expressed in its simplest terms, a leader is a person who can get people to follow him, or, as Field-Marshal Montgomery put it: 'Anyone who has the capacity and the will to rally men and women to a common cause and the character which will inspire confidence.'

Of course, a leader can be both good and bad. Hitler and Mussolini had tremendous powers of leadership, but it was an evil leadership that brought untold misery to the people they led. Leadership which is evil may temporarily succeed, but it invariably carries with it the seeds of its own destruction.

In this country today, leadership is being challenged in many fields; national, political and industrial, by many different and varied groups – youth amongst them. How many times do you hear that when something goes wrong 'it was due to a complete lack of leadership'. You see it every day in the industrial strife in this country.

This country of ours, in war, has never failed to produce leaders – the good platoon and section commanders. Why is it today there appears to be this lack of leadership, particularly amongst the younger generation? Are we teaching our young people that this country means something rather than just a welfare state? Are we teaching them that the privileges conferred upon them involve complimentary obligations, or is it just a question of all take and no give?

Since the war thousands of words have been written on the subject of leadership. Statesmen, generals, doctors, politicians have all had a go. Books have been written by the score. What was once a very simple subject is now taught as an advanced science. This to me is so much rubbish! There are many characteristics a leader may have, but there are just about half-a-dozen that are really vital. Now what are some of these?

First and foremost is Courage. Without courage no person can ever exercise the powers of leadership. As this is the vital and all-important characteristic I would like to say a word or two about it.

I do not believe that there is any man, who, in his heart of hearts, would not rather be called 'brave' than any other virtue attributed to him. This elemental and reasoning attitude is a good one. Because courage is not merely a virtue but is THE virtue. Without courage, there are no other virtues. Faith, hope and charity, and all the rest, don't become virtues unless you have the courage to exercise them.

Now there are two types of courage. There is physical courage and moral courage. Physical courage is something that every man hopes he has – it's called guts. The greatest fear, I think, any man has is when the time comes he may lack the guts to do what he may have to do.

A regiment of Gurkhas in the 14th Army were being attacked by Japanese tanks; the anti-tank weapon in those days was the PIAT, which had an effective range of about fifty yards. A young Gurkha soldier was seen to get out of his slit trench with his PIAT. He moved forward and destroyed three Japanese tanks, which caused the remainder to withdraw.

He was badly wounded and later Field-Marshal Bill Slim visited him in hospital to present him with the award of the Victoria Cross. And Bill Slim asked him why he had left his trench and moved forward. The Gurkha answered him:

'Sir, my officer told me that I was never to fire until the tanks were within a range of 50 yards. That was the only way I could destroy them.'

The Gurkha may have lacked imagination, but he certainly didn't lack physical courage.

Now for moral courage. This is an entirely different category. It is equally important and just as vital as physical courage. It is something which is much harder to exercise. It is not something that is done on the spur of the moment. It is something which is thought out and considered and which may affect a man or his family for the rest of their lives. It may involve making a decision which, even though it is the right one, could still be an unpopular one.

I'd like to tell you the story of the Reverend Theodore Hardy. This story illustrates very well this characteristic of courage. Hardy was born in Exeter in 1863, was ordained in the Church of England in 1898. In 1913 he was the incumbent of Hutton Wood, a small village in Westmoreland. When war broke out in 1914, Theodore Hardy was then aged 51. At that age he could have avoided military service without any loss of dignity or sense of failure. But no, he did not see it that way and even at the age of 51 he managed to persuade the authorities to appoint him as a chaplain to the Forces. In September, 1916, he persuaded the authorities that he must serve in France.

He became the Padre of the 8th Battalion, The Lincolnshire Regiment. In September, 1917, he was awarded the DSO for 'cool courage and self-effacing devotion to duty'. In October, 1917, he was awarded the MC for going out under shellfire on repeated occasions to help stretcher-bearers during an attack. In July, 1918, he was awarded the VC for conspicuous gallantry and devotion to duty on many occasions. His citation reads:

'Although over 50 years of age he had, by his lack of fear, his devotion to the men of his Battalion, his quiet and unobtrusive manner, won the respect and admiration of the whole division. His marvellous energy and endurance would be remarkable in a very much younger man.' It goes on to cite three specific instances of this man's outstanding bravery. His Commanding Officer said:

'His retiring nature made it almost an offence to wear the ribbons which many would have given their right arm for.' This man, who had already won three awards in eleven months, died of wounds in October, 1918 – a couple of days before his 55th birthday. I think that really brings out the courage, both physical and moral.

Another story of courage is about Lance-Corporal Hewitt of the RAMC. In North Africa the 1st Parachute Battalion were covering the withdrawal of an infantry brigade. We came to an area, surrounded by woods. We were making our way across when the Regiment brought down its artillery Final Protective Fire task on top of us.

In those days there weren't very many guns so it wasn't all that serious except when they came down on us! As one man, we took off for the woods on either side. When we turned around we saw a chap, Lance-Corporal Hewitt, who had been helping a wounded sergeant-major back. In the centre of this area there was a small hole, that was all. He dragged this sergeant-major into it and then lay down on top of him. When we went out to get them, Hewitt was dead and the sergeant-major was no worse.

Now, this was seen by the best part of three hundred chaps who said: 'If any one deserves a VC, Hewitt does'. Then I found out that Hewitt was a conscientious objector and as such he could not be awarded a medal.

Now, what is the next characteristic? I believe it is integrity. Trust is a great thing and if your men or anyone you're fighting with believe and trust you then you are ninety percent there.

The next characteristic, I think, is knowledge. Knowledge is knowing your job. Because if you have the knowledge, then that gives you the necessary confidence to do what has to be done. It also gives those you are leading the necessary confidence if they think and believe that you know your job. Knowledge gives you the power to share it and put it across. It's no use having knowledge if you cannot put it across or